STUDIES IN ANABAPTIST AND MENNONITE HISTORY

No. 15
The Theology of Anabaptism
By Robert Friedmann

Studies in
Anabaptist and Mennonite History

Edited by Cornelius J. Dyck, Ernst Correll, Leonard Gross, Leland Harder, Guy F. Hershberger, John S. Oyer, Theron Schlabach, J. C. Wenger, and John H. Yoder

Published by Herald Press, Scottdale, Pennsylvania, and Kitchener, Ontario, in cooperation with Mennonite Historical Society, Goshen, Indiana. The Society is primarily responsible for the content of the studies, and Herald Press for their publication.

°Out of print, but available in microfilm or Xerox copies.

THE THEOLOGY OF
ANABAPTISM

An Interpretation

ROBERT FRIEDMANN

HERALD PRESS
Scottdale, Pennsylvania
Kitchener, Ontario

Library of Congress Cataloging in Publication Data
Friedmann, Robert, 1891-1970.
   The theology of Anabaptism.

   (Studies in Anabaptist and Mennonite history, no. 15)
   Bibliography: p.
   1. Anabaptist. I.   Title. II.   Series.
BX4931.2.F74   230'.4'3   73-7886
ISBN 0-8361-1194-X

THE THEOLOGY OF ANABAPTISM
Copyright © 1973 by Herald Press, Scottdale, Pa. 15683
   Published simultaneously in Canada by Herald Press,
   Kitchener, Ont. N2G 4M5
Library of Congress Catalog Card Number: 73-7886
International Standard Book Number: 0-8361-1194-X
Printed in the United States of America
Design by Jan Gleysteen

15 14 13 12 11 10 9 8 7 6 5 4

IN MEMORIAM
HAROLD S. BENDER
(1897-1962)
Christian - Scholar - Friend

*It would not be so hard to believe
if it were not so hard to obey.*
Kierkegaard, Diaries

*Christianity is not child's play, . . .
to be a Christian is to be commissioned.*
Williams, The Radical Reformation

Other Books by Robert Friedmann

Mennonite Piety Through the Centuries, Its Genius and Literature. 287 pp. Mennonite Historical Society, Goshen, Indiana, 1949.

Hutterite Studies. Essays by Robert Friedmann. Collected and published in honor of his seventieth anniversary. Edited by Harold S. Bender. 338 pp. Mennonite Historical Society, Goshen, Indiana, 1961.

Die Schriften der Huterischen Täufergemeinschaften, Gesamtkatalog ihrer Manuskriptbücher, ihrer Schreiber und ihrer Literatur, 1529-1667. Zusammengestellt von Robert Friedmann unter Mitarbeit von Adolf Mais. Österreichische Akademie der Wissenschaften, Phil.-Hist. Klasse, Denkschriften, 86. Band. 179 pp. Wien, Austria, 1965.

Glaubenszeugnisse oberdeutscher Taufgesinnter, II. Mit Benutzung der von Lydia Müller gesammelten Texte herausgegeben von Robert Friedmann, Quellen zur Geschichte der Täufer, Band XII. 318 pp. Gütersloher Verlag, 1967

EDITOR'S FOREWORD

With great earnestness the Anabaptists of the sixteenth century sought to set forth in writing their understanding of Christian doctrine and life. Representative essays would include the *Vindication* of Martin Weninger called Lincki (1535), the *Account* of Riedemann (1541), the *Foundation* (1539-40) of Menno, and his *Brief Defense to All Theologians* (1552), as well as an endless stream of tracts, booklets, and polemic monographs. (See pp. 121-60 of Hillerbrand's *Bibliography of Anabaptism*, 1962.) During the past hundred years a large number of scholarly studies have been made of Anabaptism, such as those of S. Hoekstra (1863), E. Händiges (1921), L. von Muralt (1938), C. Krahn (1936), H. S. Bender (1950), and G. H. Williams (1962). Dozens of dissertations on Anabaptism have been written in this generation.

Yet the present volume is in some respects unique. It is an earnest attempt, written *con amore*, to distill the reading and meditation of a lifetime into a readable and winsome interpretation. Robert Friedmann sees Anabaptism, not as Catholic theology which has been tinkered with, nor as Protestantism taken "all the way," but as an essentially new approach to the Word of God. Assumptions in the area of theology, particularly in anthropology and ethics, which had been largely unchallenged for a millennium and a half, were rejected outright by the Anabaptists — infant damnation, for example, as well as the sacramental transmission of divine grace, the legitimacy of the church hierarchy calling on "the secular" to suppress heresy, participation in the military, and in some cases even the total rejection of capital punishment. Friedmann read widely in the literature of the Swiss Brethren, but his special love went out to the Hutterites (1528-). He read their codices and epistles with such reverence that his heartbeats coincided with theirs. With great joy he wrote and revised this manuscript, and only weeks before his triumphal passing mailed it to the SAMH editor.

Friedmann's friend and colleague, Leonard Gross, archivist of the Mennonite Church, lovingly invested untold hours in perusing the manuscript and verifying the footnote references. Elizabeth Bender read it also with a careful scrutiny of its language. Kenneth Reddig, a senior at the Associated Mennonite Biblical Seminaries, prepared the index to the volume. The Friedmann family generously supplied the subsidy which made its publication possible. Finally, I take special pleasure in thanking John S. Oyer for the useful Introduction which he prepared. We now release this study to all those interested in that narrow way to life eternal as set forth by the Lord of the church.

J. C. Wenger

Associated Mennonite Biblical Seminaries
October 16, 1972

INTRODUCTION

The Mennonite Historical Society is happy to present this monograph as a memorial to one of its foremost experts on Anabaptism, Robert Friedmann. The work represents a lifetime of more than forty years of scholarly research. Friedmann developed an interest in Anabaptist research in an almost casual manner. This is the more surprising to those of us who knew the intensity, the passion, of that interest in his most mature years. He tells us how he got into the subject after he had decided to embark upon the study of history, even though he had already prepared himself as a civil engineer.

Without having any prior knowledge of Anabaptists, Hutterites, or Mennonites, Friedmann told his seminar professor at the University of Vienna, Alfons Dopsch, that he wanted to work on Austrian Reformation sectaries. Dopsch sent him to Rudolf Wolkan, who introduced him to Hutterite epistles in the form of three Hutterite codices. Friedmann was fascinated, first by the content of the epistles and the spirit which they exuded, and then also by the form in which they came — codices. This interest grew on him until it developed into his life profession and avocation. Later he considered this chance introduction to Hutterite literature to have been providential. He tells us in his own charming manner:

What captivated my interest immediately was this kind of genuineness, or as they say today, authenticity, of these epistles. They were genuine Christian existential documents, testimonials, which profoundly gripped me right at the very beginning. I began reading and as I proceeded I began to become alerted and to note a mentality completely unknown to me hitherto. These were epistles with a new sound, a new spirit, something very different from anything I had ever read before. (*Mennonite Life*, April 1971, 82.)

His study led him to faith, as well as to a completely absorbing academic occupation. Friedmann is one of those rare persons whom *academe* led to Christian faith.

The Society issues this work as a memorial to a man who was more to us than a writer on our favorite topic. He was a warm friend and a gracious critic, always eager to support and to encourage especially the younger scholar, like myself, who had only begun to explore the field. Friedmann gave special attention to the preparation of the young scholar's *Erstlingsarbeit*, and to set its author straight with gentility and good humor when he erred. Some of us took our hegiras to his Kalamazoo Mecca, to sit at his feet, to absorb his counsel, to dispute with him, and to learn. He was tenacious in his viewpoint, even when in error. I recall how he could not be convinced that he had in fact confused Ducal with Electoral Saxony on a pre-1547 map. But he ended each exchange with his engaging laugh, which always seemed to say, "Well, although you are obviously in error, we can still be friends." In this and other ways he endeared himself to us.

The special merit of this work is that it brings together his insights over the span of his research years. In particular it draws on several pioneering studies: "Conception of the Anabaptists" (*Church History*, 1940); "Anabaptist Genius and Its Influence on Mennonites Today" (Cultural Conference, 1942); "The Two Worlds" (*Recovery of the Anabaptist Vision*, 1957); "Original Sin" (*ME*, IV); "Glaubensgut" (*Archiv f. Reformationsgeschichte*, 1964) to name a few. It does not move significantly beyond these studies in its delineation of the major themes, but in the supplying of detail it does. Here is the essential Friedmann.

His introduction to what he called "existential" Christianity in Anabaptism stamped him for life, as he himself tells us. He developed a deep spiritual kinship with the Anabaptists, in part because in his view they simply lived out their religious ideas instead of attempting to systematize their theology; they were "existential" Christians. (This may be part of the reason why he considered Hubmaier atypical — for Hubmaier was a trained theologian and therefore often expressed his theological convictions in traditional theological categories. Perhaps the fact that Hubmaier rejected the non-resistance of the Swiss Brethren and the Hutterites may have heightened Friedmann's dissatisfaction. In any case, to Friedmann Hubmaier did not altogether fit the Anabaptist mold.) Systematic theology was never one of his major interests; he never studied it formally. He tended to approach the Anabaptists rather from the vantage point of his own training in *Geistesgeschichte.*

It is precisely this approach to theology that is prominent in this work: Friedmann's insistence that Anabaptist theology is neither Catholic nor Protestant, but *sui generis*, "existential" Christianity rather than traditional theology of any kind. He saw and emphasized this aspect of Anabaptism with more clarity and fervor than any interpreter of his generation. But by the same token perhaps his weakest section is the beginning of Part III, where he himself employs the traditional theological categories in order to clarify and interpret Anabaptist thought.

This work has a number of significant strengths which immediately recommend it to the serious student of the Reformation. Friedmann writes well about Anabaptist eschatology. He does, to be sure, tend to shun the more fervent chiliasts as atypical, and also tries to keep Thomas Müntzer at a respectable distance. But he is excellent on shades of meaning within what he calls "quiet eschatology." He handles church discipline in a commendable manner, despite the paucity of evidence. His selection of Anabaptist quotations is superb, and reflects wide reading in the sources. And Friedmann adds special touches that are peculiarly his own — for example, his observation that the present-day Hutterites refused to print a millenarian hymn from one of their own seventeenth-century collections because they do not accept the millenarian view. He wrote to ask them about it.

Many people have contributed to the preparation of this manuscript for publication. The readers made various suggestions. Elizabeth Bender and Leonard Gross, both of whom had often worked with Friedmann, gave special assistance in the preparation of the manuscript; the work has, in effect, been edited by them. J. C. Wenger gave it his general supervision with judicious counsel. Gross guided the manuscript through the press, personally attending to the myriads of necessary details of a publishing enterprise. All of these friends have contributed to the publication of the book with a quality of devotion which fits the attainments of the one whom they honor by their service.

John S. Oyer

Goshen College
October 10, 1972

TABLE OF CONTENTS

INTRODUCTION

Anabaptism and Protestantism

To talk about the theology of Anabaptism seems like talking about squaring the circle. Apparently there is none, and all discussions along this line seem to miss the point. Anabaptists were allegedly simple, unlearned people who were eager to live out their primitive-Christian way of life in tension with the surrounding "world," ready to suffer martyrdom for the sake of their faith. But otherwise they seem to have been just a radical extension of general Protestantism, the main tenets of which they accepted, such as opposition to the Roman church, the principle of *sola scriptura,* the Apostles' Creed, two main sacraments or ordinances, salvation not by works but by faith, and by and large a puritanical-ascetic life following the Reformed pattern but not the Lutheran one. It has become generally accepted that theologically they were close to Zwingli, whose main views they embraced, primarily the symbolic or figurative understanding of the ordinances. With Erasmus of Rotterdam they also embraced the conviction of the freedom of the will and they completely rejected predestination and the bondage of the will.

Thus, one might legitimately question what a study of the theology of the Anabaptists [1] could achieve. Some American Mennonite scholars prefer to speak of special emphases of the Anabaptists concerning certain doctrines, assuming that other-

wise a "Protestant" foundation exists as common ground upon
which the Anabaptists also stand. [2]

It seems that such a relatively simple formula will no
longer suffice. In 1950 I tried to show that Anabaptism and
(normative) Protestantism were not of the same spirit or
genius, and that it would be more correct to separate Anabaptism from the broad stream of Protestantism (namely Lutheranism and Reformed Christianity) as we have traditionally separated Unitarians and Quakers from this stream. [3] In 1962
George H. Williams of Harvard established on the same as-
sumption a totally new picture of sixteenth-century church
history by speaking of the "Radical Reformation" (rather than
of a "Left Wing of the Reformation," as Roland H. Bainton
did) as the third church-historical phenomenon alongside the
"magisterial" or normative Reformation and the Catholic
Counter-Reformation. [4] According to this view the Radical
Reformation followed its own genius and was in no way
directly related to Reformed or Lutheran Protestantism. But
even though in a descriptive sense this picture looks rather
convincing, it still leaves undeveloped a more complete appreciation of an essential element in this third Reformation.

In 1933, Ethelbert Stauffer suggested in a highly stimulating essay [5] that it was a "theology of martyrdom" that con-
trasts this Anabaptist movement with official Protestantism to
which martyrdom appeared as something utterly extraneous.
A church of the martyrs, reminiscent of the primitive church
of the apostolic age and thereafter, is certainly a remarkable
phenomenon — but is the term "theology" valid for this
phenomenon? Was the martyr-mindedness a "theological" aspect or was it not rather a practical one which had its roots
in the radicalism of the Anabaptist stand in a world of gross
intolerance from which there was next to no escape? [6] A later
chapter will discuss this unique phenomenon of readiness for
martyrdom in more detail; here we simply assume that
martyrdom does not in itself represent a theology in the proper sense of the word, and it is certainly not *the* theology
of Anabaptism in particular.

Johannes Kühn drew up a church-historical typology in

1923 [7] in which Anabaptism and Quakerism were lumped together as the *Nachfolge* (discipleship) type of Christianity. This again is a very appropriate characterization, but neither can such an idea be called a theology. Similarly, in 1944 Harold S. Bender, in his classical essay "The Anabaptist Vision," [8] spoke of a "theology of discipleship," meaning by this term that discipleship was indeed central to the Anabaptist vision. But again the question arises whether Bender was correct in calling this a theology. He never fully explained his intuitive formulation but orally he explained to me that he called it a theology in the sense that the Anabaptists embraced a form of theology in which discipleship and all it implies had a central and normative function, as compared with the theology of main-line Protestantism, which in its concern for personal salvation has no organic place for the "brother." As far as their formulations go, we are ready to agree with Kühn and Bender. Discipleship was certainly most essential to the Anabaptist way of life, and points to a frame of mind different from that of a Luther, Zwingli, or Calvin. But again, the question remains unanswered: What kind of theology actually allows such an emphasis?

Unfortunately, an inquiry into the Anabaptist writings themselves does not yield any ready answer. It is clear that besides Balthasar Hubmaier (d. 1528), who was a doctor of theology (from a Catholic university), there were no trained theologians in the broad array of Anabaptist writers and witnesses. Hubmaier was a special type, greatly esteemed by Christian radicals but not really emulated and followed after. Many of his theological ideas crept into Anabaptist thinking, such as, for instance, his doctrine of the freedom of the will, or his teachings concerning the two ordinances of baptism and the Lord's Supper. [9] But otherwise, theology of the Hubmaier kind was by and large bypassed by Anabaptists as something it would be better not to indulge in too deeply. They may have felt that it could easily lead the faithful astray from the narrow path of discipleship which is, in principle, nontheological. In fact, the first generation of Anabaptists shows a rather different tendency, namely a reliance on the spiritualistic or semimystical awareness of the presence of the Holy Spirit in the believer which enables him to understand the Scriptures without special learning, and also to interpret them afresh, independently from other teachers. To the early Anabaptists it was precisely the lack of such spiritual immediacy which made the Reformers predominantly "theologians," that is, discursive thinkers on religious questions instead of doers of divine commandments.[10]

Later, this quasi-spiritualistic trend was more or less abandoned in favor of a stricter biblicism. But whether the latter or the former, theology was not the manifest concern of the brethren and was bypassed wherever possible. Thus it would seem appropriate to pause for a moment and pose the question: What do we actually mean when speaking of theology? Otherwise it might be difficult to elaborate on the strange fact that a religious movement as vigorous as Anabaptism was apparently lacking in theology.[11] One could perhaps say that the Anabaptists were not learned men and not trained in rational or intellectual pursuits, which, of course, is largely true. But then, rationalism or intellectualism is in itself not the qualifying element of theology, even though it is one of its elements. In my opinion, theology should not be defined by any formal attribute but rather by its content; we could then say that theology deals by and large with man's ideas about God and His relationship to man, or with man's grasp of his relationship to God. Furthermore, it deals with the ideas concerning the nature of man and his place in the God-created world. About these points any *homo religiosus* must have certain definitive ideas even if rationally undefined. In brief, it is our thesis that no genuine religious movement can exist without certain underlying "theological" ideas, even if they are not precisely formulated. Hence, neither martyrdom nor discipleship as such fits into this conception of theology; rather, they are mere derivatives from theology.

This theme is quite apparent in the difference between the Gospels and Pauline epistles in the New Testament. The Apostle Paul elaborated, often with considerable sophistication, on theological issues, in the main concerning the sinful

nature of man and his redemption through the atoning death
of Christ. On the other hand, Jesus taught primarily the expectation of the imminent breaking-in of the kingdom of
God, but otherwise did not elaborate on details of theology
in the traditional sense. In fact, He seems to have intentionally eschewed explanations of an intellectual kind. And yet,
who would dare to claim that Jesus had no theology? It appears that the difference could in part be explained by the
distinction between *implicit* and *explicit* theology. The epistles of Paul unquestionably contain an explicit theology; in
fact, most of the Pauline epistles deal with doctrinal questions, even though they are not shaped into a complete
rational system. That was done later by the Church Fathers,
in particular, Augustine. Ever since his time we can speak of
a theological system (besides formulated creeds which are
simply the precipitation of theological ideas or positions).
System is certainly a feature of explicit theology, and the sixteenth century was especially productive in the formulation
of such systems: Luther, Zwingli, Calvin, Bucer, Oecolampad,
and many others have done this.

But the other form is just as legitimate as the explicit
one: the implicit theology, unformulated perhaps, but nevertheless leaving its imprint on every word or deed flowing from
such prime insights. Thus we may speak correctly of an implied or implicit theology of the Gospels, or better still of Jesus Himself. As a rule Jesus spoke in parables, though now
and then He taught His disciples in sermon-fashion also. But
behind parables and sermons we sense the basic convictions
which scholars and schoolmen later condensed into specific
theological terms but which had been an actual part of religious life rather than religious thought. Understandably,
systems are obnoxious to those who hold to such an implicit
theology. Nevertheless, it is legitimate also to call this a
theology; it is in fact well justified if we mean by it the sum
total of these basic beliefs or insights mentioned above.

This brief analysis may help somewhat to clarify the
problem of Anabaptist theology. It is correct to say that no
serious religious movement can be thought of without an un-

derlying implicit theology, notwithstanding the lack of documents of an explicit theological nature. We have untold creedal statements or formulations by the Anabaptists, we have confessions of faith, proceedings of trials, minutes of debates, and the like — unsystematic, to be sure, and in most cases also nonrational. Usually these testimonials of faith are filled with an overabundance of biblical references, or, as Williams so graphically describes it, they often present to us nothing but a beautiful mosaic of Scripture texts.[12] All of this points back, however, to semiconscious theological insights and ideas concerning God and man and their mutual relationship, eventually expressed concretely in confessional statements. The question is nevertheless in order, why in some instances explicit theologies developed (as, for instance, in magisterial Protestantism), yet in other instances such systematic formulations are absent (as with Anabaptism). Obviously there must be a basic difference in the spiritual outlook which either leads explicitly to a theology or prevents one, or even makes it rather unwanted, indeed suspect.

To formulate sharply the difference between the two ways is not simple, and it is not our task here to analyze the New Testament writings with this question in mind: on the one hand Jesus' parables and sermons, and on the other hand Paul's *theologoumena*. In some ways the difference repeated itself on a lower level between Anabaptism and magisterial Protestantism. It has been suggested more than once that the absence of systematic theology among the Anabaptists may have had two possible causes: (1) the lack of learned men (besides Hubmaier) who could achieve such semirational elaborations and (2) the perpetual emergency situation caused by cruel persecution which allowed little leisure for the production of such a system. Neither explanation really holds true. As to the first point, there were certainly a number of men like Conrad Grebel and Felix Mantz; Pilgram Marpeck, Menno Simons, Dirck Philips, and several more who were well educated but showed little inclination toward this kind of activity although they wrote voluminously. Moreover, one could rightly ask why there were not more "learned" men to be found among the Anabaptists, save for the earliest beginning. Apparently the movement had little appeal to this type of intellectual, and it was certainly not merely accidental that no explicit theology was formulated.

As to the second point, there were doubtless also periods of quietness, for instance in Moravia, where Hutterite writers were extremely productive, but not in the field of theology. And, as has already been noted, men like Marpeck or Menno Simons wrote many volumes of religious tracts and polemics, in spite of persecution and wandering, but they wrote no theology.

Another example can be found among the anti-Trinitarians, mainly the Socinians. Some, like Servetus or Ochino, had been theologians of the first order, in spite of the fact that they spent a great deal of their lives wandering from place to place. Theology was their great passion, obviously because of their outspokenly rationalistic view of Christianity. Thus, neither of the aforementioned arguments is acceptable for the explanation of the lack of systematic, theological thinking within Anabaptism.

On the other hand, a glance at Luther, Zwingli, Calvin, Bucer, Melanchthon, Bullinger, Beza, and — excepting the Anglicans — all the other leading men of the great Protestant churches of the sixteenth century, immediately reveals that theology was basic to their total vision, their "revolution," their *raison d'être* for the break with Rome, in fact, the very center of the new idea of the church. Theology brought about within the churches a strange quality of predominance of the intellectuals — the professor — over men of the plain forms of life. The clergy had to study at theological schools in order to know how to expound the Scriptures. "Hear the sermon" was the prime requirement of a good Protestant, for "faith comes by hearing" (as Paul said); and only the learned minister is certified to expound the Scriptures properly to the helpless layman. As to life as such, the answer too was at hand: are we not completely sinners? No one can claim exemption from this human predicament. But hearing and believing the good tidings of redemption "by faith alone," we return to

God *simul justus ac peccator.* Faith, we learn officially, means lastly the trust in God's gracious promise, reliance in the atoning merit of Christ's death on the cross, and the certainty that by believing in it we all will be saved. In Reformed theology the predestinarian thesis requires additional proof of our status of election by certain ascetic forms of life which, however, do not alter the centrality of theology.

That Anabaptists on their part had been extremely critical of this very situation — above all, the separation of faith and life — is well known. For the territorial (princely) churches, no other way seemed possible; just as for the sectarian or "free" churches the sternness of their requirements was a natural consequence. They intended to be "saints," in spite of all their human frailness, and for that reason they felt less spoken to by some of the Pauline dialectics. The conflict was by no means one of works-righteousness, or a return to legalism, or perfectionism[13] versus justification by faith *alone.* The Anabaptists never taught such perfectionistic doctrines, although they stressed sanctification more than justification. The real conflict was rather one of *evidencing faith in life;* that is, a correspondence of faith *and* life, versus the Protestant formula of *simul justus ac peccator* which Anabaptists certainly could not understand at all, much less accept as scriptural.[14]

To magisterial Protestantism theology had become the very qualifying trait, just as for Catholicism the sacramental practice is its qualifying characteristic. Hence the uneasiness of Protestantism can be understood where it was faced with the Anabaptist challenge, and its calling them "teachers of works-righteousness." Protestants of the sixteenth century claimed that this Anabaptist challenge was outspokenly a form of self-righteousness, in fact, a sort of perfectionist heresy, and therefore to be repudiated. For centuries this was the prevailing judgment of the Protestant established churches and their historians.

To the Anabaptists the exact opposite was obvious: they accused the Protestant leaders of taking the life and the commandments of Christ too lightly (what today might be called the idea of "cheap grace"), and relying too much on God's graciousness without earnestly trying to be worthy of such grace. Here we clearly see the conflict in sharp relief. It was more serious than first visualized. Theology *as a system* they considered rather a stumbling block to discipleship and no real help in man's earthly predicament. To be sure, this was not a question of Christian ethics and practicing Christian virtues (which was, of course, also enjoined by the Reformers). In the last analysis it has always been an existential question, a question of either readiness or unreadiness for the kingdom of God. This reaches far beyond moral issues. At one time Martin Luther also saw this dilemma very clearly; in 1526, in his *Deutsche Messe,* he exclaimed, "But alas, where do we find people ready for this way?"[15] And by this admission he totally abandoned the idea of an *ecclesiola in ecclesia,* the church of the saints, the doctrine of sanctification.

Footnotes to "Introduction"

1. The term "Anabaptists" is limited in this work primarily to the activities and thought of the Swiss Brethren, the South and Central German Anabaptists, and the Austrian Hutterites — the Zurich beginnings of 1525 granting to this grouping an organic unity.

2. J. C. Wenger, *The Doctrines of the Mennonites* (Scottdale, 1950). Reprinted 1952.

3. Robert Friedmann, "Anabaptism and Protestantism," *Mennonite Quarterly Review* (hereafter *MQR*), XXIV (1950), 12-24. Among non-Mennonites L. von Muralt and Lydia Müller (see Bibliography) were inclined to interpret Anabaptism as a form of modified Protestantism with all the major doctrines unchanged. Recently also John H. Yoder of the Goshen Biblical Seminary took a similar position in his *Täufertum und Reformation im Gespräch* (Zürich, 1968), 3: "In bezug auf die Rechtfertigung und die sonstigen evangelischen Grundwahrheiten blieben die Täufer durchgehend mit den Reformatoren einig." ("With regard to justification and other basic evangelical truths the Anabaptists remained throughout in unity with the Reformers.")

4. George H. Williams, *The Radical Reformation* (Philadelphia, 1962).

5. Ethelbert Stauffer, "Märtyrertheologie und Täuferbewegung," *Zeitschrift für Kirchengeschichte,* LII (1933). In English: "The Anabaptist Theology of Martyrdom," *MQR,* XIX (1945), 179-214.

6. The only exceptions were Moravia for the Anabaptists, and Poland and Transylvania for the Socinians and Unitarians.

7. Johannes Kühn, *Toleranz und Offenbarung* (Leipzig, 1923).

8. Harold S. Bender, "The Anabaptist Vision," *Church History,* XIII (1944), 3-24; and *MQR,* XVIII (1944), 67-88. Many reprints.

9. Franz Heimann, "The Hutterite Doctrines of the Church and Common Life, a Study of Peter Riedemann's *Confession of Faith* of 1540," *MQR,* XXXVII (1952), 22-47, 142-160.

10. E. W. Gritsch, *The Authority of the "Inner Word"* (PhD dissertation, Yale, 1959); Walter Klaassen, "Spiritualization in the Reformation," MQR, XXXVII (1963), 67 ff. (an excellent article).

11. In contrast to the anti-Trinitarians, who seemed to revel in theological speculations of a semi-rational nature and were willing to sacrifice everything for this theology.

12. Williams, *op. cit.*, 821.

13. See the excellent article by Harold S. Bender, "Perfectionism," in the *Mennonite Encyclopedia* (hereafter *ME*), IV, 1115.

14. See Hans G. Fischer, "Lutheranism and the Vindication of the Anabaptist Way," MQR, XXVIII (1954), 36: "Luther's theological formula 'simul justus ac peccator' cannot possibly be defended; it is definitely unscriptural." Fischer is a Lutheran minister in Vienna.

15. Martin Luther, *Deutsche Messe* (1526), Weimar edition, XIX, 75.

PART ONE

Why Anabaptists Have No Explicit Theology: Anabaptism Interpreted as Existential Christianity

It seems appropriate to start with a pertinent question: Why can there not be an Anabaptist theological system? Or still better: Why can there be *in principle* no explicit Anabaptist theology? At the risk of some ambiguity, we shall try its formulation: Ever since the days of the apostolic church, Anabaptism is the only example in church history of an "existential Christianity" where there existed no basic split between faith and life, even though the struggle for realization or actualization of this faith into practice remained a perennial task. There is no claim of perfectionism as was the case, for instance, with later Pietism or Quietism; nor any claim of works-righteousness (salvation by works), which Anabaptists expressly denounced as false. But they never knew the experience of a *zerspaltenes Herz*, which is so well known in the history of the church. Claus Felbinger, a Hutterite brother, expressly repudiated it during his trial in 1560: "I know that God does not want a split heart. . . ."[1] And likewise, Anabaptists had no room for Luther's rather sophisticated formula of *simul justus ac peccator*. If God commands a way of life, the disciple has to obey unreservedly, even though the struggle with the flesh is hard and unending.

Here one may object that there might have been a great deal of self-delusion or even hidden pride with these brethren. For who can ever lay/ claim to such an inner harmony or saintliness? And further: one may easily point to the fact that Anabaptists frankly admitted facing permanent temptation toward backsliding or relapse.

The reply sounds as unusual as it is simple — an answer every regenerated person has always been willing to accept. For the Anabaptists, baptism meant a solemn vow "not to sin anymore," as Jesus admonished; to resist sin, and to walk "the narrow path" of discipleship as Jesus had urged His followers. Only the one who had experienced that unique, spiritual uplift which the Apostle John in his Gospel (3:3) described as *metanoia* — only this spiritually transformed man was ready to join, through baptism upon faith, a group such as the Anabaptists.

The price was well known to all: contempt from the many, persecution, and perhaps martyrdom. To be sure, such a position required spiritual fortitude and a unique vision which enabled the person to stand all these trials to the very bitter end.

Strange as it may appear to modern man, the Anabaptists accepted martyrdom "with shining eyes." "How does it happen," asked the Dominican monk John Fabri of Heilbronn in 1550, "that they accept death so readily and joyfully?"[2] In fact, we may inquire, how was this endless line of martyrs possible with all their readiness to stand up to their faith? By the middle of the sixteenth century more than five thousand of their group had suffered cruel death and all kinds of torture. How could it be explained, except by indulging in an easy formula such as mass hysteria or the like? Indeed in the eyes of the world it was sheer fanaticism, unhealthy and sickening. But when one reads the records of trials of Anabaptists, or their writings, their letters, their confessions, and defenses, their chronicles and farewell speeches (as one may find, for instance, in van Braght's *Martyrs Mirror* of 1660),

one senses their sanity and inner soberness, also their absolute certainty of being on the right path and of being obedient
to their God. In brief, one senses their assurance of being
authentic disciples of Christ. All this did not last indefinitely,
perhaps not more than three generations (as was also the
case with the early Christians). But when everything was
new, say between 1525 and 1550, this radical following of
Christ swept like a prairie fire all over Central Europe, and no
persecution could intimidate the multitude of committed men
and women and keep them from witnessing.

The status of rebirth was not really familiar to the Reformers; it was at best but dimly guessed: hence the basic
estrangement between the two camps and their dissimilarity.
I suggest the term "existential Christianity" for the Anabaptist camp.[3] But by this term I mean something different from
what is today often called "Christian existence," which denotes
the status of despondency and lostness, the exact opposite
of what is implied here by the term "existential Christianity."
This latter term means a realized and practiced "Christianity
of the gospel," in which the person has to a large degree
overcome the basic dilemma of every Christian believer. He
does not experience an ongoing *Anfechtung* (inner doubt),
no feeling of despair or, worse, of perdition, but rather
the exact opposite: the *certainty* of resting in God's gracious
hands, of being called and able to respond to this call. Such
a believer is intent on being obedient to God's commands and
is willing to accept the possible price. It reminds one
somewhat of the type described in the Gospel as the man who
sells everything to buy the pearl of great value. There was
no modern schizophrenia at work; unhesitatingly these disciples accepted baptism upon faith, at least during the first
enthusiastic decades of the movement.[4] Often people rushed
to places where they could hear the new message, even at
great risk, and once they accepted this "existential decision"
they stuck to it, being often compelled to leave wife and
child, house and goods, and to expose themselves to the cruel-
ties of the "world," challenging it at the same time.

As an example we present here a short testimony of

George (Jörg) Wagner, an early martyr (1527), who at the place of execution publicly stated:

> It would be a bad thing that I should suffer death for
> something which I had confessed by mouth and not also
> in my heart. I certainly believe what I have confessed.
> My treasure is Christ whom I love, and to Him also be-
> longs my heart, as He speaks: where your treasure is there
> is your heart also. And this treasure no man will ever pull
> out of my heart, nor shall any suffering or pain make me
> turn away from Him. For I have known it well beforehand
> that I shall have to carry the cross when I follow Him. No
> idol shall possess my heart, and it is the dwelling place of
> my Lord.[5]

Or to quote another shining example, the defense of Claus Felbinger, who in 1560 was sent out on a mission trip to Bavaria. "I am certain in my faith," he said before his judge, "God be thanked. I have no doubt that I am on the right path. I find no error in my heart and I know for sure that I rest in the true grace of my God."[6]

These are just two examples: whoever studies the records meets similar testimonies on nearly every page. What is so extraordinary about these testimonies is the matter-of-factness of their words. No tragic pose, no big words, simply the admission that it was to be expected that the world would contradict the way of faithful discipleship at all times.

Existential or Concrete Christianity. It was Søren Kierkegaard who first brought this term into circulation, visualizing "the Christianity of the New Testament," in contrast to organized church-Christianity. But he unfortunately added that such Christianity simply did not exist. At least he could not see it anywhere in his time. His words were an open challenge to the various established state churches of the day. He was not interested in church history but merely observed the shallowness of contemporary official Christendom. It was in his most significant essay, *Concluding Unscientific Postscript* of 1848, that he elaborated on the new term "existence" and "actuality," as opposed to "objectivity" in matters of religion. To Kierkegaard it meant the rather difficult task of becoming "subjective," explaining that in his understanding "faith is the highest passion in the sphere of human subjectivity" or inwardness. Truth (meaning religious truth), he tells us, is basically such an inward subjectivity, an inner experiential awareness, not vague but concrete. God is known to us foremost in this state of subjectivity. Otherwise — in the form of objectivity — God could easily become an idol. Existential certainty is then the direct opposite of speculative thought. Since the latter presents itself usually in the form of a "system," Kierkegaard comes to the profoundly convincing conclusion that an *existential system is impossible.*

Thus, a theological system cannot be existential, and existential Christianity cannot be pressed into a theological system. This sounds oddly ironic, all the more since today there is so much talk about existentialism in theological circles. In fact, there prevails a certain haziness concerning these terms. Modern theologians like to quote Kierkegaard, and then they speak of anxiety and despair, loneliness and man's sinful predicament as "existential" situations of a Christian; they speak of "Christian existence" as the unsettling calamity of man today. Obviously this is something completely different from the claim made above concerning Anabaptist testimonials as examples of existential Christianity, meaning the unity of faith and life, and the very absence of that despair and anxiety even in the face of death.

And yet, only thus can we understand the absence of theology as a system among the Anabaptists (or, for the sake of comparison, among the early disciples and apostles). A theological system would contradict the very nature of this way of witnessing. The Anabaptists were always willing "to give account of the hope that is in you" (1 Peter 3:15), but they were not willing, nor even able, to construct a systematic theology, a rational edifice of thought. It would be foreign to them and inadequate to the "subjectivity" of the new birth.

That seems to be the deepest reason why Anabaptists had no explicit theology and why on the other hand Anabaptism appeared so extraneous to the Protestant way and style of life and thought. There were numerous debates

between Protestant theologians (mainly Zwinglians) and
Anabaptists in Switzerland up to about 1540,[7] there were
important disputations such as the one at Pfeddersheim,
1557, or the well-known Frankenthal Colloquy· of 1571,[8]
but there was actually very little real communication even
on these occasions. The inner rebirth made a difference in
the level of thought and experience. *Anfechtung* (tempting
doubts concerning the certainty of faith and its truth), so
typical particularly of Lutheran thought, hardly mattered for
the Anabaptists. They were absolutely certain of their way
and of their God. In fact, they felt already in a state of
redemption which more or less eliminated for them the necessity of speculating about the question "how to find a gracious
God." In their basic orientation Anabaptists were not
guided primarily by Pauline ideas, as was the case with the
Reformers. Actually, the classical *loci* of Lutheran or Reformed theology are rarely found in Anabaptist writings.

To demonstrate the existential nature of Anabaptism by
way of quotations is of course not easy as the words used
come from a different vocabulary. Thus, for instance, they
use the term "living faith" (*lebendiger Glaube*) where
today we might speak perhaps of "existential" or "concrete"
faith. "Baptism," to quote Felbinger, "makes no one more
God-fearing (*fromm*) unless he has already a living faith."[9]
A. Orley Swartzentruber fittingly used the term "authentic
language" for what he discovered in many of the early documents of *Martyrs Mirror,* such as the writings by Michael
Sattler, Anneken Jans of Rotterdam (1539), Leonhard Schiemer,
and others.[10]

In fact, the entire "theology of martyrdom," which Ethelbert Stauffer documented so well, becomes explicable only on
the foundation of "existential" faith, which carries absolute
certainty concerning divine truth and the accompanying divine
call, even in face of death. These men and women knew
themselves to be redeemed persons who had attained a certain consciousness of salvation or divine grace in the here and
now. They felt as if they were already in God's womb; hence
they were no longer worried about man's constitutive corrup-

tion and lostness. If it were otherwise, they might rejoin, how could God ask man to *obey* His command and to be a disciple? If God asks and commands, then it must be possible for man to do it, and it will not be beyond his capacity in Christ. That does not mean in any way "works-righteousness," legalism, or Judaizing. It means simply to try to be obedient in a childlike way, out of an inner freedom of decision. And they are sure that even suffering for the sake of one's faith will never go beyond man's ability to endure it manfully and trustfully. But one thing is needed which the scholar (*Hochgelehrter*) does not automatically possess or appreciate: the simplicity of the heart (*die Einfalt des Herzens*).

The disciple knows very well that the "world" will contradict him; in fact, that is the very first thing he will understand after the truth has been explained or revealed to him prior to his baptism. But he also understands that an "untested faith" is no real faith at all. "As gold has to be tested in fire, so faith has to be proven in tribulation,"[11] the Anabaptists are fond of quoting, as well as Ecclesiasticus 2:5: "For it is in fire that gold is tested, and men agreeable to God are tested in the oven of tribulation" (cf. 1 Peter 1:7 and 4:12, also Proverbs 17:3).[12] This is an ever-recurring motif in their writings and defenses. The real test, however, comes always in the form of the "cross," or "baptism with blood" (1 John 5:8).

To be sure, this idea of suffering as the testing ground of faith is something very different from Thomas Müntzer's (and later pietists') "theology of the cross" (*Kreuzestheologie*) where suffering is understood as the normal situation of a believer, as the *Heilsweg eines Menschen in Anfechtung*, with all his calamities and doubts.[13] In contrast, the Anabaptists conceived their idea of testing mostly under the figure of the "suffering church" or brotherhood of believers, bound to be contradicted by the world. Essentially it is a primitive Christian concept.[14]

The documents of Anabaptist thought overwhelmingly and eloquently reveal this existential character of their faith, just as the writings of the New Testament show essentially the same quality of mind. There is no trace of doubt as to one's faith, and there is this amazing matter-of-factness in their witnessing, their strange courage and undauntedness both at trials and at the place of execution. "I search myself every day," wrote Claus Felbinger, "but I find no error in my faith. For I know that I stand in the grace of God."[15] That is it. It may sound strange, perhaps even a bit foolish, in an age of agnosticism, but such is the nature of the Christian faith when actually lived out in practice.

Footnotes to "Part One"

1. W. Wiswedel, *Bilder und Führergestalten aus dem Täufertum*, II (Kassel, 1930), 130. The complete text of Felbinger may be found in Johann Loserth, *Der Communismus der Wiedertäufer in Mähren* (Vienna, 1894), our quotation, p. 173. The entire document is worth reading.

2. *ME*, II, 286. The complete title of Fabri's pamphlet reads as follows: *Von dem Aydschwören. Auch | von der Wiedertäuffer Marter, Und woher es entspringt, dass sy also frölich and getrost die pain des todts leiden* (Augsburg, 1550). (Translated: "Concerning the Swearing of Oaths; also Concerning Anabaptist Martyrs; and the Source of the Reason Why [the Anabaptists] so Joyfully and Confidently Suffer the Pain of Death.")

3. I am neither the first nor the only one to use this characterization. Beatrice Jenny used it in *Das Schleitheimer Täuferbekenntnis,*1527 (Schaffhausen, 1951), 40, where she writes: " . . . eine bestimmte Lehre, aber sie hat keinen Eigenwert, weil das Christentum der Täufer ausschliesslich *existenziellen Charakter* hat, und die spekulative Seite der Theologie sie nicht interessiert." Harold S. Bender employed this term in his essay, "The Anabaptist Theology of Discipleship," *MQR*, XXIV (1950), 31. Likewise A. Orley Swartzentruber in his most excellent study, "The Piety and Theology of the Anabaptist Martyrs," in van Braght's *Martyrs Mirror*," *MQR*, XXVIII (1954), 21. Friedmann had already used the term in his "Anabaptism and Protestantism," *MQR*, XXIV (1950), 19, although without further development.

4. E.g., Fritz Blanke, *Brothers in Christ* (Scottdale, 1960), German (Zürich, 1955), where a dramatic description is offered of the first Anabaptist "Gemeinde" at Zollikon near Zürich, in 1525.

5. W. Wiswedel, *op. cit.*, 114. Wagner was actually not an Anabaptist in the strict sense of the word but his testimony is quoted here nevertheless as a good illustration of what we mean with the term "existential Christianity."

6. *Ibid.*, 128. Also Loserth, *op. cit.*, 173.

7. See John H. Yoder, *Täufertum und Reformation in der Schweiz*, I: *Die Gespräche zwischen Täufern und Reformatoren 1523-1538* (Karlsruhe, 1962), where an elaborate description is presented of all these debates.

8. See "Disputations," *ME*, II, 70-74, which is very enlightening.

9. Wiswedel, *op. cit.*, 125. The German text is even more expressive: "Die Taufe macht niemanden frömmer, wo nicht schon ein lebendiger Glaube ist."

10. A. Orley Swartzentruber, *op. cit.*, 131. Swartzentruber used the expression "authoritative language," whereas he really meant "authentic" language.

11. Andreas Ehrenpreis, *Ein Sendbrief...*, 1650 (new edition, 1920), 92. The same simile appears with Leonhard Schiemer, 1527, Hänsel Schmidt, 1558, and the Great Article Book of 1577. It is common possession of the Anabaptists.

12. See Leonhard Schiemer's writings in Lydia Müller, *Glaubenszeugnisse oberdeutscher Taufgesinnter* (1938). In his "Von dreyerley Gnade" (1527) he writes: "Es bedarf einer guten Schmelzhütten, einer starken Prob, eines scharfen Scheidewassers, denn ein ungekreuzigter Christ ist wie ein unprobiertes Ärtz" (67). In his tract, "Von dreyerley Tauff" (also 1527), Schiemer writes similarly: "Denn ein unprobierter Christ ist gleich wie ein unprobiertes oder ungeschmoltzenes Ärtz"; and: "Der im Schmelzofen des Trübsals geprüfte Glaube" (78).

13. See O. Brandt, *Thomas Müntzer, sein Leben und seine Schriften* (Jena, 1933), 29: "... Gott sendet seinen Auserwählten das [innere] Kreuz." See also Müntzer's *Protestation und Entbietung, 1524, ibid.*, 142. The expression "Heilsweg eines Menschen in Anfechtung" I borrowed from John H. Yoder, *Täufertum und Reformation im Gespräch* (Zürich, 1968), 194.

14. The expression "suffering church" appeared for the first time in Conrad Grebel's famous letter to Müntzer, September, 1524. See Bender, *Conrad Grebel* (1950), 202, 205; the text, in Williams, *Spiritual and Anabaptist Writers*, 1957, 80, 84; also in J. C. Wenger, *Conrad Grebel's Programmatic Letters of 1524* (Herald Press, 1970), where the original handwriting is reproduced, together with a transcription, a translation, and an introduction.

15. Wiswedel, *op. cit.*, 128. See footnote 6.

PART TWO

The Heart of the Implicit Theology of Anabaptism: The Doctrine of the Two Worlds; Kingdom Theology

In spite of all that has been said up to this point, the Anabaptists definitely had a theology of their own, although different from that which we traditionally ascribe to Protestantism, as first formulated by Luther, Zwingli, and Calvin. Theology may be very different under different assumptions, and the Anabaptists were never very conversant with traditional Protestant thought. They did not read much in Luther, Zwingli, or Calvin; and likewise they were hardly familiar with the Church Fathers except perhaps to the extent that Sebastian Franck, their trusted contemporary, quoted them.[1]

The Bible alone was the guide to their newly found faith, and this Bible (in either the Lutheran or the Zurich edition) they read assiduously from cover to cover, including the Apocrypha. To them it was an open book, and they claimed to have experienced a spirit akin to it. They read it as people seeking divine guidance. They read it without sophistication, to be sure, rather unaware of tradition — medieval, sectarian, or otherwise. However, Grebel, Hubmaier, and Hans Denck probably knew a bit of Erasmus.[2] The overwhelming rank and file of Anabaptists, however, were simply students of the Scriptures and hardly of anything else.

To the Hutterites Hubmaier was a kind of authority, mainly with regard to his arguments against infant baptism, concerning the meaning of the Lord's Supper, and of course because of his defense of the freedom of the will. To some extent Hans Denck, and particularly Hans Hut, were also respected teachers, as the many copies of their writings in Hutterite codices or in the *Kunstbuch* of 1561 show. But in the last analysis the basic theological ideas had to be grasped by each believer individually from Scripture. No external authority would matter for this kind of existential belief.

In order to reconstruct the implicit theology of these people, an unconventional approach is needed which bypasses most formulations of present-day theology. A goodly number of "normative" Christian theologies are thinkable. There exists, to begin with, a tripartite biblical tradition: the Pauline, the Petrine, and the Johannine. Then there are the theologies of the Church Fathers, both Greek and Latin, culminating for the West in Augustine. Later, the schoolmen developed several theologies, such as the Thomist, Scotist, and Occamist, and in addition a number of unorthodox systems developed in the course of the centuries. Finally, Protestantism developed at least two great "Augustinian" theologies — those of Luther and Zwingli/Calvin.

Inasmuch as the Anabaptists strictly limited themselves to the study of Holy Scriptures, only the first-named possibility applied to them, namely the Pauline, Petrine, and Johannine traditions. Peter, it seems, comes the nearest to the genius of the Synoptics (which count the most in Anabaptism), and Anabaptist writers show an obvious preference for Petrine ideas, namely, for quotations from the epistles of Peter. "Baptism," we read here, is "the answer of a good conscience to God" (1 Peter 3:21). This is one of the most frequently quoted passages in Anabaptist writings. Other Petrine ideas include: "Ye are a royal priesthood" (2:9); "Rejoice, inasmuch as ye are partakers of Christ's suffering"

4:13); "Be ready always to give answer to every man that
asketh you a reason of the hope that is in you" (3:15), a
quotation Riedemann put on the title page of his great
Rechenschaft of 1541; "Charity shall cover a multitude of
sins" (4:8); "But the end of all things is at hand" (4:7); and
"Look for a new heaven and a new earth" (2 Peter 3:13).
We also read the remarkably frank admission in 2 Peter that
there are some statements in Paul's epistles "which are
hard to be understood by the unlearned" (3:16), a statement
shared unhesitatingly also by the unlearned Anabaptists.[3]

This general observation, however, does not suggest
that the brethren were basically "Petrine" Christians. They
were disciples and followers of Jesus Christ, who took most
seriously His call "to take up your cross and follow me."
Existentially, by way of prime spiritual experiences, they
most likely understood Jesus better than they understood
Peter, Paul, or John, even though they quoted amply from
all of these, in addition to the Old Testament, and their beloved Apocrypha. This leads us to the larger question, that
of the implicit theology of Jesus Himself, as represented by
the Synoptic Gospels, couched, to be sure, in parables and
informal talks. Obviously, we cannot deal with this question
in all its many aspects. It concerns us only insofar as it applies to Anabaptists who by inner consent had accepted the
message of Jesus. That such a theology must go beyond the
idea of discipleship is certain; yet it is also certain that
discipleship assumes an integral function in it, as opposed
to any "normative" theology (primarily Protestant) where
such a function is missing. What would be the nature of such
a theology?

The answer I propose penetrates to the very center of
the quest. It consists basically of two related parts.

First we recognize in Anabaptist writings the acceptance of a fundamental New Testament dualism, that is, an
uncompromising ontological dualism in which Christian values
are held in sharp contrast to the values of the "world" in
its corrupt state.[4] A few of the many possible quotations from
Anabaptist sources may serve to illustrate this idea, so

unfamiliar to modern man. The *Schleitheim Confession of Faith* (1527) says in its Third Article:

All those who have fellowship with the dead works of darkness have no part in the light. All who follow the devil and the world have no part with those who are called unto God out of the world. All who lie in evil have no part in the good.

And in the Fourth Article:

For truly, all creatures are in but two classes, good and bad, believing and unbelieving, darkness and light, the world and those who have come out of the world, God's temple and idols, Christ and Belial, and none can have part with the other.[5]

Still more elaborate on this rather philosophical point is the anonymous Great Article Book of the Hutterites, written most likely by the Bishop Peter Walpot around 1577. Section Four, Point 70, of this book reads as follows:

Between the Christian and the world there exists a vast difference like that between heaven and earth. The world is the world, always remains the world, behaves like the world and all the world is nothing but world. The Christian, on the other hand, has been called away from the world. He has been called never to conform to the world, never to be a consort, never to run along with the crowd of the world and never to pull its yoke. The world lives according to the flesh and is dominated by the flesh. Those in the world think that no one sees what they are doing; hence the world needs the sword [of the authorities]. The Christians live according to the Spirit and are governed by the Spirit. They think that the Spirit sees what they are doing and that the Lord watches them. Hence they do not need and do not use the sword among themselves. The victory of the Christians is the faith that overcometh the world (1 John 5:4), while the victory of the world is the sword by which they overcome [whatever is in their way]. To Christians an inner joy is given; it is the joy in their hearts that maintains the unity of the Spirit in the bond of peace (Ephesians 4:3). The world knows no true peace; therefore it has to maintain peace by the sword and force alone. The Christian is patient, as the apostle writes (1 Peter 4:1): "As Christ hath suffered . . . arm yourself likewise with the same mind." The world arms itself for the sake of vengeance and [accordingly] strikes out with the sword. Among Christians he is the most genuine who is willing to suffer for the sake of God. The world, on the contrary, thinks him the most honorable who knows how to defend himself with the sword.

To sum up: friendship with the world is enmity with God. Whosoever, therefore, wishes to be a friend of the world makes himself an enemy of God (James 4:4). If to be a Christian would reside alone in words and an empty name, and if Christianity could be arranged as it pleases the world; if, furthermore, Christ would permit what is agreeable to the world, and the cross would have to be carried by a sword only . . . then both authorities and subjects — in fact, all the world — would be Christians. Inasmuch, however, as a man must be born anew (John 3:7), must die in baptism to his old life, and must rise again with Christ unto a new life and Christian conduct, such a thing cannot and shall not be: "It is easier," says Christ, "for a camel to go through the eye of a needle than for a rich man (by whom is meant here the authorities in particular) to enter the kingdom of God or true Christianity" (Matthew 19:24).[6]

Such a dualism of heaven and hell, Christ and Belial, was most characteristic of late Judaism (said to have been influenced by Persian thought), particularly of the Essenes of the Dead Sea Scrolls, and of early Christianity. It was also basic for all the "Old Evangelical Brotherhoods,"[7] such as the Bogomils, Cathari, and Waldenses. In the sixteenth century it even appears with Erasmus of Rotterdam and with Carlstadt, whose influence upon Hubmaier is beyond doubt.[8] It became the mainstay of the Anabaptists of practically all shades — hence their withdrawal from the world and their challenge to the world.

This dualism is, of course, not the heart of their implicit theology. There must be a supplementary doctrine, an idea which would allow both a dualism and also discipleship as constituent elements and not only as marginal consequences.

The answer comes very simply if we look closely at the two sides of this dualism. We see the tension between the kingdom of God (or kingdom of heaven) on the one hand and the kingdom of the prince of this world (or the kingdom of darkness) on the other. If the reborn believer decided for the former kingdom, his "theology" was clearly marked. It is generally known as *kingdom theology*. It is the hidden theology of Jesus Himself and His deepest message.[9] "Be prepared," He says (Matthew 24; Mark 13; or Luke 21), "the kingdom is imminent. But only the pure will enter into it, while all the rest will perish." This is definitely an eschatological idea, and requires some effort to decide either for or against "the world." Yet it is a glorious idea and far superior to any worldly philosophy, a promise not of a "yonder" after death, but of a present possibility.

This kingdom theology fits almost perfectly to everything said above. It requires a close brotherhood of committed disciples as the citizens of the expected kingdom.[10] It also implies discipleship as basic, and finally makes the believer aware of the eternal warfare between the "children of light against the children of darkness,"[11] roughly corresponding to the aforementioned "theology of martyrdom."

It is obvious that the mood, piety, and other aspects of life are affected by whether one lives by kingdom theology with its dualism of "Christ/world" or by the traditional theology of "salvation by faith alone," with its own dualism of gospel and law. As had been the case with early Christianity so it was also with the Anabaptists: they were filled with a strong expectation of the kingdom soon to break in, and they were also aware that such a kingdom cannot be entered into except by separation from the world and by a radical turn toward a life of brotherly love and purity. By this the believer was preparing himself to become worthy of the kingdom. The Christ/world dualism is meaningful, however, only if the Christian withdraws to his island, that is, to what he considers a partly realized kingdom of God, where there is no more hatred and violence but only brotherly sharing and peaceful togetherness. By a continuous struggle against all that is negative in one's nature, man's self-image is changed and he conceives of himself as a child of God with a great task ahead. This picture of a child of God was most central in the Anabaptist self-understanding. It also prevented any form of pietistic servility in their outlook. Considering themselves as such children of God, they willingly accepted all subsequent hardships in the world in "childlike obedience."[12] Peter Riedemann was right when he called this new situation a "covenant of childlike freedom."[13]

All this must have sounded like sheer fanaticism, if not downright hypocrisy, to outside observers. Did these people, they would ask, not know the curse of "original sin"? Obviously, the existential situation of the rank-and-file Christians of the sixteenth century was basically so different from that of the Anabaptists that any fruitful dialogue or understanding between the two camps had become impossible. Vis-a-vis the eternal questions, however, "natural man" found himself in a grave predicament and confusion. Thus he accepted readily the main doctrines of "normative" Protestantism: that salvation comes through faith only, and that faith comes by hearing the Divine Word. Accordingly, he was taught to rely exclusively on the expounding of Holy Writ by learned clergymen to whom he had to listen regularly on Sunday. Existentially, however, that did not really alleviate the deeper conflicts between faith and the practical demands of life. "The good I would I do not," he exclaimed with the Apostle Paul (Romans 7:19), "but the evil which I would not that I do." Resentment to the Anabaptist challengers was only too natural.

With the Anabaptists things were apparently different. The presupposition underlying their way was an existential event of tremendous power, namely the inner or spiritual regeneration, the "new birth" or (with John 3:3) *metanoia*. By this event man is transformed; gaining insight into the world of the Spirit and its values. It denotes a lifting-up of the mind by which the world of common sense loses its dominance. A reorientation occurs which makes man less willing to yield to the temptations and enticements of the "natural world," such as warfare, adultery, greed, and the like. In place of the feeling of deep insecurity of the average churchgoer,[14] the reborn experience a feeling of security, of resting in God's grace, and of being a new man who, though he will suffer with Christ, will also rise with Christ on the new day. In brief, the Anabaptist knows something of the good conscience of which Peter wrote.

We have no reason to doubt that at least during the creative period of the Anabaptists, experiences of this kind were real and genuine. Both their behavior and their writings witness to it.

But, the question is still legitimate whether this interpretation, the emphasis on kingdom theology, is adequate and final. It may be argued that the term "kingdom of God" does not appear too frequently in Anabaptist documents. But then we may point to their unique and most concrete idea of the *Gemeinde*, the brotherhood-church, otherwise unknown in the Protestant world. It is a gathering of the reborn, an attempt to translate the kingdom idea into practical forms of everyday living — if not in terms of the fullness of the kingdom itself, then at least in what it foreshadows. That alone makes sense of the withdrawal to remote locations such as Moravia, Russia, the American West, and even Paraguay, where one could serve one's God without compromise.

The kingdom idea also implies a collective witnessing which is a tremendous help to each participant in his neverending fight against sin and temptation. In fact, the brotherhood is greatly needed to give strength for this fight. Should a brother ever get weak and succumb to temptations of all sorts, then the *Gemeinde* will apply its disciplinary provisions according to Matthew 18:15-18, from brotherly admonition to possible ban and exclusion. After all, that is the "rule of Christ," or "the rule of the kingdom." No other rule is needed. Conrad Grebel used this term as early as 1524 in his letter to Thomas Müntzer: "The Lord's Supper should not be used without the rule of Christ in Matthew 18:15-18, for without that rule every man will run after the externals. The inner matter, LOVE, is passed by if brethren and false

brethren eat [the Lord's Supper] together." And again: "Go
forward with the Word and establish a Christian church with
the help of Christ and His rule."[15]

One more point remains to be discussed, namely, the inner dynamics of the ideas here developed — in particular
the dynamics in the idea of *Nachfolge*. Once the reborn person comes to know that God has revealed to him His will,
there is but one thing for him to do: to obey. The word
"obedience" is used more often in Anabaptist writings than
the term "discipleship," or following Christ. The brethren are
fond of referring to Paul's somewhat radical admonition "to
bring into captivity every thought to the obedience of Christ"
(2 Corinthians 10:5), a demand obviously not too easily
obeyed.[16] The logic, however, of this demand to follow in
the footsteps of the Lord is rather simple and, to the Anabaptists, convincing. If God gives commands in His Scriptures,
they are meant to be obeyed and not only to be looked
at as something unattainable and paradoxical. Beginning with
Hubmaier, the Anabaptists were conscious of their inner
freedom, not as "natural" persons, to be sure, but as reborn
ones.[17] They were free initially either to accept or to reject
God's command. Early Anabaptists speculated only about the
kind of obedience expected of them, whether it was to be a
"childlike obedience," hence joyful and acceptable, or a "ser-
vile obedience," hence legalistic and obnoxious.[18] But no
Anabaptist would ever have thought of justifying his failings
by saying: "Because Adam fell and with him all mankind, I
am not free." Judging from the records, freedom of the will
was a tacit precondition of *Nachfolge*.[19]

But then, what about the doctrine of man's basic corruption? This will be more elaborately discussed below. Suffice
it to say here that no Anabaptist ever claimed to be sinless.
He knew only too well the danger of "backsliding" or failing
due to weakness and temptations, and was willing to accept
brotherly discipline. But the possibility of aberration as such
could be no valid counter-argument against the previous existential decision to walk the narrow path and to recognize
it as the true task of a Christian.

Once the new birth was sealed by the rite of adult baptism, confidence was established that God would lend sufficient strength to the faithful to overcome what is corrupt in him and he will no longer find pleasure in it. "Such a faith," said Hubmaier (in 1524), "does not like to stay idle but must break out in thanksgiving toward God and in all kinds of works of brotherly love toward man."[20] Not despair but obedience to the divine law is expected of the discipline. In a marginal note to the tract *Von der Freiheit des Willens* (1527), Hubmaier says simply and straightforwardly: "To a godly man the law is not a law but a guide on the way."[21] Obviously, such a way could not be walked alone. Only in the togetherness of a living brotherhood could the faithful realize *Nachfolge* — a bit of God's kingdom.

This is the theological or spiritual framework of the life of an Anabaptist. This was his strength but also his very real limitation. And these limitations we certainly must not overlook either. It is almost a truism to say that most of the values of Western civilization — aesthetic, scientific, and philosophical — do not fit into this dualistic vision and the implicit hope for the kingdom. Thus it came about that Anabaptism actually existed at the edge of civilization (which in a strict sense can never be "Christian"). The Renaissance, Baroque, Enlightenment, Rationalism, and the philosophy behind the Scientific Revolution — in brief, the entire history of "Modern Man" — remained outside the Anabaptist realm. All these movements were to them secular happenings which had no bearing on the kingdom of God. This attitude can still be observed today with both the Amish and the Hutterite brotherhood churches, the last remnants of original Anabaptism.[22]

A strange paradox is hidden in Anabaptist history. As long as the spirit is strong and vital, the course of this history is meaningful and creative, in spite of persecution, and maybe even in reaction to it, inasmuch as persecution forestalled any easy way out. Once, however, the spirit passed, as it was bound to do just as it passed after the Apostolic Age, new developments set in — perhaps doctrinal orthodoxy, or a rigid legalism, or even secularism. Among the descendants of the Anabaptists there was hardly ever a tendency toward a doctrinal orthodoxy, inasmuch as there was no explicit theology. But legalism or formalism was certainly a temptation for later generations when a tradition had crystallized, allowing the illusion of still being loyal to the origins while in reality preserving only certain external forms.

This development helps to explain why for the man of the twentieth century it appears so difficult to appreciate the genius of Anabaptism as it existed at the time of its flowering. Such dualism is to modern man a rather unfamiliar "philosophy," and save for a few marginal figures the idea of the kingdom has lost much of its appeal. But in studying the numerous records and tracts of the past a most meaningful picture emerges, and gradually we begin to understand what was intended. Anabaptism had embarked on a great venture "to seek first the kingdom and its righteousness"; as regards all the rest the brethren did not worry. This injunction sounds familiar enough to the man of our century. But not familiar at all is what it implies in terms of concrete acts and a most real suffering. Here we are in need of new vistas.

Footnotes to "Part Two"

1. The Anabaptists were acquainted, however, with Eusebius, whose history of the martyrs was congenial to the Anabaptists.

2. See also Thor Hall, "Possibilities of Erasmian Influence on Denck and Hubmaier in Their Views on the Freedom of the Will," *MQR*, XXXV (1961), 149-170. This is a very good paper.

3. The statistical tabulation seems to belie this statement. John A. Hostetler in his *Education and Marginality in the Communal Society of the Hutterites* (Pennsylvania State University, 1965), Table 3, presents a tabulation of all the 2,950 Bible references in Peter Riedemann's *Rechenschaft* of 1541. He found that the Gospel of John was referred to 285 times; the Epistle to the Romans, 256 times; Matthew, 222 times; 1 Corinthians, 140 times; Hebrews, 109 times; Ephesians, 97 times; and the First Epistle of Peter, only 94 times; etc. However, such statistics are misleading. One has to weigh the references as to their significance. Only then will the genius of such a work be revealed. But weighing defies tabulation.

4. This dualism must not be confused with the well-known Pauline dualism of "spirit" and "flesh," or Luther's dualism of "gospel" and "law." The specific Anabaptist dualism of Christ/"world" I had suggested for the first time in my essay, "The Doctrine of the Two Worlds," in G. F. Hershberger, ed., *The Recovery of the Anabaptist Vision* (1957), 105-118; also included in my *Hutterite Studies* (1961), 92-102.

5. See J. C. Wenger's translation of the Schleitheim Confession, *MQR*, XIX (1945), 249 ff. Reprinted in Lumpkin, *Baptist Confessions of Faith* (Judson Press, 1959, 23-31), in Manschreck, *A History of Christianity* (Prentice-Hall, 1964, 79-82); Hillerbrand, *The Reformation* (Harper & Row, 1964, 235-238); Hillerbrand, *Protestant Reformation* (Harper, 129-36); Leith, *Creeds of the Churches* (Doubleday, 1963, 281-292).

6. R. Friedmann and Lydia Müller, *Glaubenszeugnisse oberdeutscher Taufgesinnter*, II (1967), 252. First referred to in *Archiv für Reformationsgeschichte* (hereafter *ARG*), 1931, 211.

7. See R. Friedmann, "Old Evangelical Brotherhoods: Theory and Fact," *MQR*, XXXVI (1962), 349 ff.

8. See Hans J. Hillerbrand, "The Origin of Sixteenth-Century Anabaptism: Another Look," *ARG*, LIII (1962), 160, 165, 167. Carlstadt advocates a *Gelassenheit* approximating that of the Anabaptists.

9. See Rudolf Otto, *The Kingdom of God and the Son of Man* (2nd Engl. ed., 1943). This is one of the finest studies of the spiritual milieu of the time of Jesus. Many a feature is reminiscent of the milieu of the Anabaptists.

10. Most likely it was the same with the Essenes of Qumram long before the coming of Jesus.

11. *The War Between the Children of Light and the Children of Darkness* is one of the remarkable discoveries among the Dead Sea Scrolls of the first century BC, representing an extreme form of dualistic thinking. Michael Sattler used the term "divine warfare" too in his well-known letter to the brotherhood-church at Horb, 1527. He favored the active attitude of "fighting the beast" in contrast to the passive acceptance of suffering. His witnessing at his trial was such a "warfare."

12. "Two Kinds of Obedience: An Anabaptist Tract on Christian Freedom," translated and edited by J. C. Wenger, *MQR*, XXI (1947), 18-22.

13. Peter Rideman, *Account of Our Religion* . . . (1950), 68, in the chapter "Concerning the New Covenant." See also *MQR*, XXVI (1952), 214. ("Rideman" is now generally spelled "Riedemann.")

14. This insecurity feeling was acutely experienced centuries later in Pietism, when it was called *Sündenangst*, or dread of sin.

15. Quoted from the English translation in George H. Williams' *Spiritual and Anabaptist Writers* (1957), 77, 79.

16. There is a difference in translation between the King James version (which

has: "captivity of *thought*") and the Lutheran translation which says: " . . . und nehmen gefangen alle *Vernunft* unter den Gehorsam Christi." A good illustration of the Anabaptist usage of this reference may be found in a letter "to a weak brother" by the outstanding early Anabaptist, Hans Schlaffer (*ca.* 1527): "Man soll sich nicht zu sehr besorgen, wenn man gewisse Geheimnisse der Schrift nicht versteht. Man sollte eher seine Gedanken in die Gefangenschaft des Gehorsams Christi nehmen." Lydia Müller, *Glaubenszeugnisse* . . . (1938), 107; see also Hans Hut, *ibid.*, 19.

17. Hubmaier seemed to have been influenced in part by Erasmus. See the study cited in note 2.

18. "Two kinds of Obedience. . . ." *MQR, loc. cit.*

19. See "Free Will," *ME*, II, 387-389.

20. Balthasar Hubmaier, *Schriften*, ed. Bergsten (1962): "Achtzehn Schlussreden," 1524, 72.

21. *Ibid.*, "Von der Freiheit des Willens," 1527, 393. The German gloss reads as follows: "Darum ist dem Gottseligen das Gesetz nicht ein Gesetz sondern eine Wegweisung." The English translation of the tract by George H. Williams (see above, footnote 15) omits this gloss.

22. An exception are the Dutch Doopsgezinden (Mennonites) of the seventeenth century and their relatives in East Prussia and Danzig. In the Netherlands the Doopsgezinden showed an intense interest in the values of the secular world, mainly in art and poetry (Rembrandt, Vondel, etc.), and often they lived in comfortable affluence and bourgeois respectability, much in contrast to their South German, Swiss, and Austrian coreligionists. But by that time old-fashioned Anabaptism was no longer operative among the Dutch. The bourgeois life had worked in a new direction where piety and moral decency replaced the original drives of the great beginnings.

PART THREE

What Anabaptists Have to Say Concerning Traditional Theological Categories

Introduction

If we grant that our interpretation of Anabaptist "theology" as kingdom theology, as developed above, is correct, we have said more or less all that matters. We have formulated the vital center of Anabaptist thought, and one may assume that all the rest is then but marginal. Is that really true?

As we have already seen, the traditional forms of theology do not fit the framework of Anabaptist thought. Theology, however, has to be conceived of as being broader than the conventional categorization of religious experience. But how? That poses at once the problem of theology within the history of Christianity. Two quotations of recent origin may illustrate this problem, one by an expert on the Old Testament, and another by an Anabaptist scholar from the Reformed tradition.

G. Ernest Wright of Harvard strongly felt the inadequacy of conventional categories when studying one of the most "existential" religious documents available: the Old Testament. "Theology," he said, "is the discipline by which the Church translates Biblical faith into the nonbiblical language of another age."[1] Of course he was speculating here on the difference between Hebraic and Hellenic theology. At the center of "biblical" theology, he tells us, stands a *confession of faith* and not a system of categories. We may safely say that the same applies equally to Anabaptism, explaining in part why it is so difficult to recognize in its documents the implied theological ideas.

Similarly, Beatrice Jenny, in her analysis of the Schleitheim Confession of Faith of 1527,[2] emphasizes the existential character of this document, and asks whether the Anabaptists were not actually closer to the New Testament than the learned theologians of their day. And then she reflects on a remark by Eberhard Griesebach, who in an academic lecture on "Christianity and Humanism" (1938), remarked: "In its encounter with Greek philosophy Christianity became theology. That was the fall of Christianity." This is certainly a frank admission that rational theology is foreign to the Bible.

Both quotations suggest that we must always distinguish between theological and existential thinking. This likewise applies to the attempt of clarifying the "theological" content of Anabaptist testimonials. Would the use of the traditional, in fact scholastic categories and classifications of theology, with such chapters as Christology, anthropology, soteriology, and so on, mean a distortion of the original ideas? There is no easy answer. Jan J. Kiwiet, in his study of Pilgram Marpeck,[3] criticizes such attempts to classify Marpeck's theological ideas into scholastic divisions, claiming cogently that such an analysis misses the basic pathos of the Anabaptist venture, and to some degree even falsifies Marpeck's ideas.

Traditional categories of dogmatic theology must under no condition replace the very center of an existential faith, whether Hebrew, early Christian, or Anabaptist. On the other hand the question of how to proceed in elucidating the Anabaptist mind with regard to the many theological issues encountered has not yet been adequately answered. Any person with a deep religious or spiritual outlook is bound to face sooner or later a number of questions concerning life, the world, and eternal destiny, which cannot be bypassed simply by referring to existentialistic formulations. Even though the Anabaptists were not interested in the intricacies of Greek theology or Augustinian-Protestant dogmatics, they were at all times confronted with such unsolved questions. They had to answer them in debates with opponents or at court trials where theologians often tried to make them recant by sophisticated arguments. Even in their mission work they faced questions of this kind time and again. Naturally they would have preferred to answer all such inquiries "confessionally," with a simple "we so believe,"[4] or by saying, "Come and live with us, then you will know." But in most cases that obviously did not suffice.

Theological questions were even pressing within the brotherhood. "What do we teach," some younger members would ask their elders, "about sin and about divine grace?" What does Christ and His life mean to us? What is the nature of man? Is he ever capable of obeying God, or is he not rather corrupt to such an extent that discipleship remains a utopia, a false ideal?[5] Thus the Anabaptists were inevitably led to develop ideas concerning all the traditional questions or categories of theology, not in spite of their different presuppositions but on account of them. They could not borrow much from Zwingli, and even less from Luther. The core idea of the kingdom of God carried with it a number of possible consequences such as withdrawal from the "world," close brotherhoods, eschatological readiness, and above all an awareness of a "good conscience" toward God, all of which was tacitly understood when converts joined the brotherhood. But the complex of traditional categories had to be clarified, nevertheless. And thus, in spite of our own reluctance to press existential Christian visions into nicely compartmentalized chapters, we shall nevertheless have to embark on a new and subtle analysis of that kind. We will have to come to terms with such questions as what the Anabaptists had to say about God, the Trinity, and Christ; about man lost and redeemed; and what they taught concerning salvation, justification, and grace. Eschatology was to them a particularly proper topic within the context of their basic presuppositions. And finally "ecclesiology," a learned term for something very near at hand: the idea of *Gemeinde* — or even better *Gemeinschaft* of the brethren — was of preeminent significance to them all.

Thus we shall use these age-old categories for this analysis, well aware of the inherent limitations, and the complexity of the subject. We do not plan to build up a new system, enticing though it might appear. But we hope to clarify implicit ideas of the Anabaptists along such guidelines. Since there is no official creed, confession, or catechism, valid for all the groups, we have no other way to proceed than by selecting random, representative statements or testimonies, preferably from the earlier period. Soon we discover the inner consistency of these documents, and at the same time also their basic difference from traditional dogmatics. We thus propose to discuss Anabaptist teachings according to 1) their ideas concerning God, the Trinity, and the nature of Christ; 2) their original anthropology (after all, man is not only a sinner but also a disciple); 3) their soteriology, including the delicate problem of grace within the Radical Reformation; 4) their eschatology, which has to be studied in greater detail; and finally 5) their ecclesiology, together with a glance at their understanding of the two ordinances of baptism and the Lord's Supper. All this is admittedly a novel enterprise but the results, we hope, will in the end be worth the effort. A great example of Christianity, lived and witnessed to, will reappear before our eyes.

Footnotes to "Part Three: Introduction"

1. G. Ernest Wright, *God Who Acts* (1952), 108, and *passim*.
2. Beatrice Jenny, "Das Schleitheimer Täuferbekenntnis, 1527," *Schaffhauser Beiträge zur vaterländischen Geschichte* (28. Heft, 1951), 40.
3. Jan J. Kiwiet, *Pilgram Marbeck . . .* (Kassel, 1957), 85.
4. E.g., Franz Heimann, in *MQR*, XXVI (1952), 35, where he analyzes Peter Riedemann's *Rechenschaft*.
5. John H. Yoder in his *Täufertum und Reformation im Gespräch, op. cit.*, 20, quotes Zwingli as saying: "Human nature is never capable of doing good, not even in a Christian person." Obviously, the Anabaptists taught the exact opposite, vigorously denying that the Apostle Paul's lament in Romans 7 represents a normal model of Christian experience.

Theology: Apostolicum, Trinity, the "Bitter Christ"

Few topics within the theology of the Anabaptists are relatively as uncomplicated and plain as the topic of theology proper: the doctrine of God, or more specifically, of the triune God. It has to do with a creedal affirmation which the non-speculative Anabaptists accepted without difficulty. Such an affirmation was not central within their existential approach, and in their own group they hardly ever referred to it. But in "confessions of faith" presented to the authorities, they often began with this topic to confirm their strict creedal orthodoxy. In brief, they accepted the *Apostolicum* as a whole without hesitation, since it did not in any way interfere with their own particular concern for discipleship and the building up of the kingdom. Whether we look at Riedemann's great *Rechenschaft* of 1541, submitted to the Landgrave Philip of Hesse, or at Leonhard Schiemer's "Twelve Articles of Our Christian Faith" of 1527,[1] or at the "Confession of Faith" of an unknown brother around 1540,[2] or the like, it is always the same: a more or less elaborate confirmation of the traditional Apostles' Creed, the starting point of most Christians, including Catholic, Protestant, and Orthodox. In the same sense we can safely say that the Anabaptists were orthodox concerning the very foundations of their Christian faith.

Far more difficult to them was the discussion concerning the Trinity. Of course, they were Trinitarians beyond doubt, in fact they were quite sensitive when confronted with anti-Trinitarian ideas.[3] On the other hand, confessing anti-Trinitarians were not infrequently called "Anabaptists,"[4] thus confusing the main line of descent. When in the Netherlands the celebrated case of Adam Pastor arose — the unique event of an Anabaptist turning anti-Trinitarian (1547) — the Doopsgezinden knew very well how to handle it: excommunication.[5] Or when, around 1570, Polish anti-Trinitarians sought contact and friendship with Hutterites in Moravia (whose

communitarian way of life had impressed them) the Hutterites made it quite plain that there could be no real fellowship between the two groups. In fact Peter Walpot, then the
bishop of the Hutterites, refused to call them "brethren."[6]
Though the Anabaptists did not emphasize trinitarian doctrine, they definitely did affirm it, opposing any deviation.
"Trinity" is not a biblical term, hence to the biblicistic
Anabaptists it was an unfamiliar concept, all the more as
the elaborate "hellenic" speculations of the first three centuries on the subject of "three persons but one substance" were
extremely foreign to the nonspeculative brethren. In a very
remarkable "Letter to a Weak Brother" (1527) Hans Schlaffer
answers the worries of a troubled inquirer very simply:
"God is neither this nor that,"[7] thereby quoting a line of a
hymn by Ludwig Haetzer:

> Ich bin auch weder dies noch das,
> Wem ichs nicht sag, der weiss nit was.[8]

Another Anabaptist brother, Hans Betz of Eger, while
imprisoned with many others in the dungeons of Passau, in
1535, composed a number of hymns, one of which deals
with the Trinity. It is included in the oldest hymnbook of the
Anabaptists, the famous *Ausbund*, as the eighty-first hymn.
One of its stanzas says:

> Vernimm die göttliche Dreyheit
> Wird beschlossen in Einigkeit
> Woll in der Sonnen reine.
> Die zeigt uns drey Würckung in eyn,
> *Licht, Stral und Hitz thun dise sein.*[9]

In the doctrinal writings of the Hutterites we find at least
two significant passages dealing with the Trinity, although
they do not probe too deeply into the hermeneutics of the
doctrine. Peter Riedemann in his *Rechenschaft* of 1541, apparently following Betz's picturesque symbolism says:

For as fire, heat and light are three names and yet but one

substance . . . even so are God the Father, Son, and Holy
Spirit three names yet one being. . . . Just as breath
determines the word and gives it shape and sound, so does
the breath, wind, and Spirit of God make the word living
and active within us.[10]

The *Handbüchlein wider den Prozess* (c. 1558), Book
Nine, also has a significant passage on the Trinity, to be sure
in a nonspeculative fashion. The author is unknown, but
probably the later bishop Peter Walpot was at least co-respon-
sible for the text:

We say with Paul that Christ according to the flesh derives
from the seed of Judah and David, but according to the
Spirit he is God Himself, blessed in all eternity. . . . We
will not deviate from the doctrine of the Eternal Son and
the Holy Spirit, neither with works nor with words, and
would rather suffer death to the glory of God through Jesus Christ.[11]

The last great defense of the Trinity is found in the highly
interesting correspondence the seventeenth-century Hutterite
bishop Andreas Ehrenpreis carried on with three Danzig
members of the (anti-Trinitarian) Polish Church in which
Ehrenpreis tried to convince them of the correctness of the
Trinitarian doctrine. These epistles (extant only in codices in
Hutterite Bruderhofs), although long and elaborate, add little
to the basic orthodox thesis of the sixteenth-century Hutterites.[12]

Christology. Turning to the doctrine of the nature of
Christ, we again find among the Anabaptists almost no interest in such speculation. The Chalcedonian doctrine was accepted unreservedly without further ado. Thus we read, for
example, in the confession of faith of Ambrosius Spittelmaier
(1527): "Christ, true God and true man, the head of all His
members, . . ."[13] But one feels that this is not the center,
the decisive element in this faith which took hold of the believing Christian and made him accept martyrdom. What truly
mattered was both the model life of Christ and the fact of
His death on the cross. It was not the glorified Christ, whom

Schwenckfeld emphasized so strongly, but the "suffering servant" in His agony, who became the true Lord of the brethren.

The peculiar distinction between the "sweet" and the "bitter" Christ, as Müntzer had earlier formulated it,[14] was valid also for Anabaptist thinking. To them it was the "bitter Christ" who mattered most, even though this Müntzerite term was not common among Anabaptists. Hans Hut, for instance, "preached Christ crucified, showing that Christ was obedient to the Father in suffering unto death."[15] And this element of suffering emerges more and more as a central point in Anabaptist thinking: the "suffering church" (Conrad Grebel), "redemptive suffering" (Hans Hut), and similar terms are part of their ideological framework. "The world truly accepts Christ as a gift," writes Hans Haffner (1535), a Philippite brother in Moravia, "but does not know him at all as the suffering Christ (*leidenderweis*)."[16] Without this awareness of the Son of God crucified, the entire "theology of martyrdom" would fall. And it is this martyr-mindedness which gave Anabaptism its particular quality and character.

But Christ was also the model or example of the "way" or "narrow path" in life. Time and again we read of "following the footprints (*Fussstapfen*) of the Master." And as He loved man, so has also the disciple to love man; as He gave Himself in utter humility, so has the disciple to deny himself likewise and become humble. All speculative, basically "hellenic" sophistication of patristic theology is left behind. Christ is "the Lord," and that alone mattered.[17]

Footnotes to "Theology"

1. Müller, *Glaubenszeugnisse*, 46-58.
2. Hans Hillerbrand, "Ein Täuferbekenntnis aus dem 16. Jahrhundert," *ARG*, L (1959), 40-54.
3. This fact needs underscoring because not only the Jesuit, Dunin-Borkovski, but others as well saw strains of anti-Trinitarianism in Anabaptism. See Stanislaus v Dunin-Borkovski, "Quellenstudien zur Vorgeschichte der Unitarier des 16. Jahrhunderts" in *75 Jahre Stella Matutina* (Feldkirch, 1931), 91-138. For a general evaluation, see Friedmann's article "Dunin-Borkowski," *ME*, II, 109.
4. Roland Bainton expressly counts Servetus among the Anabaptists. Stanislaus Kot writes about "Anabaptists" in Wilna (Lithuania), 1563 ff., *ARG*, 1958, 212 ff.; George H. Williams is more discriminating, making a distinction between the early Polish anti-Trinitarians before Faustus Sozzini whom he calls "Anabaptists" and the later Polish Church after the arrival of Sozzini. See his "Anabaptism and Spiritualism in the Kingdom of Poland. . . ." *Studia nad Arianizmem* (Warsaw, 1955), 216-262.
5. Henry E. Dosker, *The Dutch Anabaptists* (Philadelphia, 1921), has a very enlightening chapter on the Pastor case.
6. See R. Friedmann's comprehensive study, "The Encounter of Anabaptists and Mennonites with Anti-Trinitarianism," *MQR*, XXII (1948), 139-162; also Friedmann, "Reason and Obedience, an Old Anabaptist Letter (1571) and Its Meaning," *MQR*, XIX (1945), 27-40.
7. L. Müller, *Glaubenszeugnisse*, 108.
8. Josef Beck, *Geschichtsbücher der Wiedertäufer in Oesterreich-Ungarn*, (Wien, 1883), 34. See also the *Mennonitisches Lexikon* (hereafter *ML*), II, 231. Goeters, who deals with this passage, claims that this noncommittal formulation corresponds to a passage in Chapter 30 of the then very popular *Theologia Deutsch* and its "theologia negativa." See J. F. G. Goeters, "Ludwig Haetzer, a Marginal Anabaptist," *MQR*, XXIX (1955), 260. The claim by some writers that Haetzer was himself an anti-Trinitarian is challenged by Goeters. Inasmuch as Haetzer was hardly more than a "Randfigur" in Anabaptism, this issue would not change any point of our discussion.
9. *Ausbund, das ist etliche schöne Lieder, wie die in der Gefängnuss zu Passau in dem Schloss von den Schweitzer Brüdern und andern rechtgläubigen Christen hin und her gedichtet worden*. The oldest edition: *Etliche schöne christliche Geseng*, etc., 1564; an enlarged edition, 1583. Hans Betz's hymn is the first one in the 1564 edition, and in all later editions, hymn 81.
10. Peter Rideman, *Account of Our Religion, Doctrine and Faith*, etc., Eng. edition, 1950.
11. Wiswedel and Friedmann, "The Anabaptists Answer Melanchthon," *MQR*, XXIX (1955), 218, 219.
12. See "Zwicker, Daniel," *ME*, IV, 1051. For the larger picture, see R. Friedmann, "Encounter. . . .," note 6 above. Leonard Gross is pursuing a study on Ehrenpreis' "Christology," the results of which hopefully will be published in the near future.
13. Herbert C. Klassen, "Ambrosius Spittelmayr: His Life and Teachings," *MQR*, XXXII (1958), 256. See also *Täuferakten: Bayern I*, ed. Schornbaum, 1934, p. 51.
14. See "Sweet and Bitter Christ," *ME*, IV, 668 f., by Robert Friedmann.
15. Herbert Klassen, "The Life and Teachings of Hans Hut," *MQR*, XXXIII (1959), 186.
16. Robert Friedmann, "Concerning the True Soldier of Christ, etc.," *MQR* (1931), 92.
17. It is worth noting that the emphasis with Anabaptists is on the lordship of Christ rather than on the idea of Christ as "Redeemer" (as with normative Protestantism). More will be said on this subject in the chapter on soteriology. See also Harold Bender's address, "Christ Our Lord," at the *Seventh Mennonite World Conference*, 1962, reprinted under the title, "Who Is the Lord?" in *MQR*, XXXVIII (1964), 152-160.

B

Anthropology:
Body, Soul, Spirit; Man Between Sin and Love

Far more exciting than the topic of the first chapter is
the subject of this second chapter, the eternal question raised
by the psalmist: "What is man?" (Psalm 8:4). With the fall of
Adam, as we have been taught by theologians ever since
Augustine, all men became corrupt and inherited "original
sin." Accordingly, we live in a state of depravity and deserve nothing but hell. Man, we also learn on high authority,
has no freedom of the will but is bound by the decree of
God Almighty. Only through the redeeming death of
Christ is man freed and entitled to the hope of salvation.
Thus traditional Protestant anthropology centers nearly
exclusively on the idea of sin and sinfulness: What is man?
A sinner. . . .

Anthropology, or the doctrine of man, is crucial also for
the Anabaptists; but it remains our task to discover the
proper formulation of it, which obviously differs radically
from the briefly sketched Protestant position. Were man's
plight so hopelessly fated as described, then all the endeavor
of following Christ (discipleship) would be meaningless and
futile. Hence, a new and radically different start has to be
made. For that we take for our lead the learned Dr. Balthasar Hubmaier. To be sure, Hubmaier himself had no disciples,
as far as a church was concerned. But his writings exerted
the profoundest influence on incipient Anabaptism. He was
the theologian of the first-generation Anabaptists in South
Germany and Austria.[1] Only he was sophisticated enough
to develop an anthropology appropriate for Anabaptist self-
understanding, and — as we may add — a most original one.
It is true that Hubmaier is not too often referred to in Anabaptist tracts. Yet one senses his ongoing influence in studying
such writings. Riedemann and Walpot among the Hutterites
are good witnesses to this point.

The best elaboration of Hubmaier's anthropology may

be found in his very profound tract *Von der Freiheit des Willens,* 1527.[2] We find therein an interesting tripartite or trichotomic anthropology, following the biblical hints in Genesis 2:7 and 1 Thessalonians 5:23. Hubmaier distinguishes three elements in man: body, soul, and spirit. The body derives from the clay God used in making man, and the spirit was aroused by God's breathing into Adam's nostrils. The soul, however, stands between them, but is most of the time in servitude to the flesh, the body.[3] Torsten Bergsten calls our attention to the fact that Luther also was familiar with this age-old idea but radically opposed it. In his *De Servo Arbitrio* he expressly called it "the fable of Origen."[4]

The flesh, we read in Hubmaier's tract,

> is worthless and good for naught, but the spirit is happy, willing, and ready for all good. The soul, sad and anxious, standing between the spirit and the flesh, knows not what to do, is blind and uncomprehending as to heavenly things in its natural power. But because it has been awakened by the Word of God . . . made whole again through His dear Son, now comes to know what is good and evil, and has recovered its lost freedom. . . . If the soul is obedient to the Spirit, it becomes a spirit itself.[5]

By this tripartite distinction Hubmaier has the tool to blame the soul for its corruption but to exonerate the spirit from all blemish. He thus allows a new avenue for a positive interpretation of human existence. The spirit of man "has remained utterly upright and intact before, during, and after the Fall."[6] And this then is the connecting link by which we humans may grasp divine grace and divine commandments and become restored to the full image of God. As Hubmaier says in his *Christliche Lehrtafel* of 1526: "The image of God is not altogether erased in us,"[7] arguing against Romans 7:18. Thus no total depravity is ever possible; in fact, the very core of man has remained uncorrupted and able to grasp God's grace and goodness. Of course, he admits that "we are poor and miserable sinners,"[8] but through divine grace the original freedom of man has been restored, even if imperfectly. [9] If we surrender ourselves to God in childlike obedience, then we are truly free and able to do God's will, and thus we become disciples of Christ.

This, in brief, is also general Anabaptist teaching concerning man as found nearly everywhere in Anabaptist writings, whether by Grebel or Marpeck, by Hutter or Menno Simons, and many others. Our inborn sinfulness is no unconquerable barrier to this task; for sin — that is, original sin — must never be understood as a kind of fate. Something in man has remained unspoiled and good, and "the fall of the soul is remediable through the Word of God,"[10] referring to Psalm 19:7.

This freedom, to be sure, burdens man with full responsibility for his acts. And yet it must never be understood as Pelagianism, the alleged moral freedom of natural man. Caspar Schwenckfeld accused Marpeck of such Pelagianism, but Marpeck passionately denied it.[11] The "freedom of the will," which Hubmaier, and all Anabaptists, taught, is only the freedom of the "reborn man," the freedom under divine grace. It is never something purely "moral." Hubmaier, the first teacher of such freedom among Anabaptists, was of course well acquainted with Erasmus' *Diatribe . . . De Libero Arbitrio* of 1524,[12] but this fact should not be overemphasized, in light of the underlying differences between the Humanists and the Anabaptists.

The trichotomic anthropology implies also a threefold "will": the will of the flesh which shuns suffering and seeks pleasure, the will of the soul which would rather not suffer but cannot help suffering, and the will of the spirit which is eager and ready to suffer — typically Anabaptist.[13]

Thus the picture of man in general, as accepted by the Anabaptists, contains a hopeful aspect and avoids reliance on the pitfall of a "cheap grace" doctrine. If God commands His way, man must be able to obey such commandments after experiencing rebirth and the restoration of man's freedom in God's image. That is the essence of discipleship. Adam's fall wrought "temporal" death for all men; this aspect, Anabaptists taught in a strictly orthodox fashion. But this in turn did not cause "eternal death," inasmuch as man through Christ's sacrifice on the cross has been restored to sonship and may now become master over temptation and sin.

Man Between Sin and Love

In addition to the much discussed element of sin, there is also the positive element of man's existence: namely, LOVE. *Love is the countervailing force to sin:*[14] "Hold unfailing your love for one another, since love covers a multitude of sins " (1 Peter 4:8). Why have most theologies overlooked this positive element in the dynamics of man's life, lamenting only the inner corruption of our bodily existence? Ever since Augustine the fact of man's sinfulness has been so overstressed that the significance of love has nearly been lost. Man's existence seems hopelessly entwined in the "snares of sin." First Corinthians 13 at times may be the basis for a good sermon, or Romans 12, but theologically these passages seldom hold very much weight. The conception of human existence (or the "human situation") held by the Anabaptists, who studied foremost the Synoptic Gospels and who knew no Augustinian theology at all, will be the subject of the rest of this chapter on Anabaptist anthropology.

(A) *The Case of Sin; in Particular, Original Sin*

Original Sin. The term "original sin" is not a biblical one, as the Anabaptist Ulrich Stadler points out in one of his beautiful epistles of 1536/7: "The word *Erbsünde* (hereditary sin) has no foundation anywhere in Holy Scriptures, in fact has not been written in it at all."[15] And to counter this gloomy and fatalistic doctrine Stadler characteristically refers a few lines later to 1 Peter 2:2, "that we ought to be pure as newborn babes who know neither good nor evil."[16]

But even though Anabaptists were not ready to yield to this doctrine of original sin with its far-reaching implications, they encountered the issue time and again in debates and court trials where their opponents asked how anybody could ever deny the curse of the events of Genesis 3, which fell on all mankind. Inasmuch as the Anabaptists were really unfamiliar with the Augustinian tradition,[17] their only knowledge of this doctrine derived, strangely enough, from the pseudo-epigraphical *Fourth Book of Esdras*,[18] which dates back to about AD 100 or later: "O thou Adam, what hast thou done! For though it was thou that sinned, thou art not fallen alone but all of us that come of thee" (7:48). This book, generally not known to English Bible readers, was well known to readers of the Vulgate and apparently also quite popular with sixteenth-century German readers. Michael Sattler quoted it at his trial in 1527, and Peter Riedemann referred to it several times in his *Rechenschaft* of 1541 This book was very likely the main source of Anabaptist familiarity with the idea of original sin. The Anabaptists probably read little of Luther's theology, in which this doctrine is so central that on this basis alone all of his subsequent theses were developed.

This may explain why the Anabaptists held to a rather "strange" theology of sin, otherwise unknown in Christian tradition. In Sebastian Franck's famous *Chronica, Zeytbuch und Geschychtsbibel* of 1531, we find the interesting observation:

Concerning original sin nearly all Anabaptists teach as follows: Just as the righteousness of Christ is of no avail to anyone unless he makes it part of his own being through faith, so also Adam's sin does not impair anybody except the one who makes it a part of his own being and brings forth fruits of this sin. For as foreign righteousness does not save anybody, so will foreign sin not condemn anybody either. On the other hand, if Adam's sin condemns all men at once by its inherent nature, it necessarily follows that Christ's righteousness would save all men at once. But if Christ's righteousness saves only those believers who by faith have become transformed into Christ, that is, who no longer live in themselves but Christ lives in them, then it follows clearly that Adam's sin likewise condemns only non-believers who became Adam not by the mere fact of having been born but by their particular faith, or rather unfaith, and by the fact that they bring forth fruits of this kind of faith. In other words, that they are rooted and planted in him and he in them. That is how they speak of that matter.[19]

One senses that as a good and sensitive reporter Franck had engaged in talks of this kind, and that he knew many of the Anabaptists quite well.

Earlier in his work, Franck had this to say:

> Nearly all Anabaptists consider children to be of pure and innocent blood and they do not consider original sin as a sin which of itself condemns both children and adults. They also claim that it does not make anyone unclean except the one who *accepts* this sin, makes it his own and is unwilling to part with it. For they claim that foreign sin does not condemn anybody, and in this they refer back to the Eighteenth Chapter of Ezekiel. (fol. 446)

The passage reads as follows: "The soul that sinneth, it shall die. The son shall not bear the iniquity of the father, neither shall the father bear the iniquity of the son: the righteousness of the righteous shall be upon him, and the wickedness of the wicked shall be upon him" (Ezekiel 18:20, which in turn refers to Deuteronomy 24:16). In brief: inheritance of a misdeed is ineffective. This is what Anabaptists would answer their theological opponents. There is no basic fatalism (or, for that reason, excuse) in the Anabaptist approach to man's deepest corruption.

Anabaptists accepted the Genesis 3 interpretation of man's temporal death. But this has not determined man's eternal destiny. "There is a difference," the Hutterite, Claus Felbinger, explained to the inquiring authorities when arrested in 1560, "between *having sin* and *committing sin*."[20] Only the latter brings eternal harm to the soul. Hence there is only one word of admonition, not to natural man (who would not understand it) but to the regenerated, reborn man; it is derived from Paul's advice to Timothy: "Fight the good fight of faith" (1 Timothy 6:12). That was the essence of the Anabaptist outlook on life; it finds expression in vary-

ing terms in nearly all the sources. It was good scriptural
teaching.[21]

Anabaptists were, of course, not unmindful of man's predicament vis-a-vis good and evil. Jacob Hutter speaks clearly
of the *anklebende Sünde* (sin which adheres to our nature) and
our inborn weakness,[22] but he warns at once that "we
should not allow that sin to dominate in our mortal body."
This warning is repeated again and again, leading to the observance of discipline within the brotherhood. The admonition is found in the catechetical instructions to candidates for
believers' baptism. One of the important *Taufreden* (second
half of the|sixteenth|century) says: "For God in His Word com-
mands that one should desist from sin. Whosoever wants to be
a child of God must no longer touch the impure. If people
then say, 'But we are poor sinners and are unable to do the
good,' we answer that this is nothing but the counsel of the
serpent."[23]

Quite remarkable is also a treatise on "original sin" in
the *Handbüchlein wider den Prozess*, of 1558[24] of Hutterite
origin, answering in the name of all Anabaptists the accusa-
tions of the *Prozess* by Lutheran theologians assembled at
Worms in 1557.[25] This tract distinguishes (Chapter Seven)
three kinds of *Erbsünde*: (*a*) The fall of Adam, which carries
among its consequences temporal death (not implying "damnation" of innocent children, however). (*b*) Inclination to sin,
called *Neiglichkeit*, which from early youth stirs all human
hearts toward evil acts: "But we say nevertheless that if this
inclination is not acted upon, it does not work for eternal
death." It will be overcome by the power of the Lord. Finally
(*c*) the inheritance of original sin "has no power over the
believer in Christ (1 John 3:9). Such a one will guard himself
and will fight sin."[26] It means that the believer simply does
not yield to temptations, or still better, that he does not
acquiesce in it. In view of Hubmaier's anthropology such advice makes good sense even psychologically.

As we now turn from this more theological discussion
to a study of the *existential* situation connected with human

tendencies toward a life not divinely inspired (usually called "natural life"), the first question to be considered is: What did Anabaptists understand primarily under "sin," biblicists as they were? There are three, or perhaps four, definitions.

(1) The most widespread interpretation ever since Paul is the equation of "sin" with "flesh": concupiscence or lust.[27] This was apparently also Luther's understanding. The urges of the flesh are certainly innate in every creature; it all depends how one looks at them. The men of the Old Testament understood these urges as a divine commission to procreate Hence it was a divinely ordained function and no sin at all. Biblicist Anabaptists therefore approved of married life, declining any thought of monastic celibacy. A Hutterite Bruderhof in particular would have looked very much like a monastery were it not for the fact that it was composed of families usually with a fairly large number of children. Still, the temptation to yield to these urges (perhaps outside of wedlock) required watchfulness and even more, strict observance of discipline. In this regard an epistle of Ulrich Stadler, written in 1536, is most revealing in its frankness and simple formulation: "If man had remained pure and good as he was created by God, then also insemination would have proceeded without lust or evil desires. But now it is not so. God, however, winks at our marital work (*eheliches Werk*) for the sake of the children and does not hold it against those who act in fear of God and discipline."[28] This is a reference to the apocryphal Book of Tobit (8:9), where Tobit prays to God in an apologetic mood: "Thou knowest that I have not taken this my sister for a wife for the sake of evil lust but only that I may beget children by whom Thy holy name may be praised and extolled." (This reference may still be heard in Amish sermons.) Basically, it was the attitude of nearly all Anabaptists toward sex.[29]

Jacob Kautz argued in a similar vein during the beginning years of the Anabaptist movement. On June 13, 1527, he challenged his opponents to a public debate, outlining his views in seven theses, which in the traditional fashion, he nailed to the door of the Predigerkirche of Worms. Thesis Seven reads as follows: "The external eating of the prohibited

fruit by Adam would not have hurt Adam nor his descendants
if it had not been accompanied by an inner acceptance at
heart."[30] Thus everything concentrates on the inner acceptance
of the fruit. We are here reminded of Luther's famous advice
to Melanchthon, the *pecca fortiter:* "Accept it, but believe in
God's forgiveness of sinners." That was certainly not the Anabaptist way of looking at these facts. The admonition, found
again and again in the tracts of the Anabaptists to restrain
and fight temptation, usually means, like Ulrich Stadler's advice, to subdue lust and to discipline the body; without, however, eliminating what is natural and acceptable to God.

(2) But sin may also have wider connotations. Galatians 5:
19-21 lists a catalog of "sins" or vices, and it is no accident
that one of the first Anabaptists in Switzerland, Georg Blaurock,
enumerates them when he speaks of "guzzling, whoring, committing adultery, gambling, practicing usury."[31] These are
evil deeds rather than evil thoughts. That the latter are not
mentioned in our texts is no surprise. People delighting in
evil thoughts would hardly accept baptism on faith with all
that the pledge implied. The *intention* for a saintly life was
taken for granted whenever a person asked for membership in
this exclusive brotherhood.

(3) The very center, however, of this discussion of what
sin meant to the brethren existentially lies deeper than concupiscence or disorderly conduct. Sin in its deepest sense means
disobedience to God, a reliance on self-will and self-
righteousness. Peter Riedemann has this to say in his great
Rechenschaft of 1541, our most reliable source: "Sin is the
forsaking of obedience to God. For as through obedience all
the righteousness of God cometh through Christ, so also
cometh all sin and unrighteousness from disobedience to and the
forsaking of God's command."[32] Hence the disciple has to
learn one thing above all: the art of self-abandonment (in
German called *Gelassenheit,* yieldedness or resignation).[33] The
man who through yieldedness seeks to follow Christ along
the narrow path has to overcome all self-centeredness and has
to open his heart to a loving — and subsequently, usually
suffering — attitude.

Most revealing in this context is another passage of the Hutterite *Taufreden* originating in the era of the great bishop Peter Walpot (d. 1578). Here we read: "If someone should not know how to take upon himself the cross of Christ, he need only do penance and desist from all sinful life of this world,[34] and he will have his cross upon him; he need not worry any further about it."[35] A marginal gloss has this to add: "On this earth we are bound to carry the cross. If we are not willing to carry the cross of Christ, we have to carry the cross of the devil. Blessed be the one who accepts the cross of Christ."[36] This, we should say, is typically Anabaptist teaching, in marked contrast to theology as taught generally by both Catholics and Protestants.

(4) Theoretically there could be still a fourth interpretation of "sin," which contains much meaning to modern man but hardly ever occurred to the Anabaptists of the sixteenth century, namely the understanding of sin as pride or *hybris*. Reinhold Niebuhr was its main interpreter in our day.[37] It cannot be denied that such "pride" is a real, in fact existential experience of the Promethean element in man, the pride in self-reliance and autonomy. It began as a general phenomenon with the age of the Renaissance and at present has become more dominant than any other attitude of "disobedience." To the reborn disciple of Christ, on the other hand, such a frame of mind was utterly foreign. Otherwise the brotherhood would have confronted its members with unbearable conditions of life. For its ideal was always self-surrender, the direct opposite of pride and self-reliance. Moreover, the brethren were not unmindful of the many scriptural warnings against precisely such an attitude, such as, for instance, in Proverbs 16:18 (haughty spirit) or 2 Peter 2:10 (self-will and presumptuousness), and many more. It was this Renaissance pride which is largely responsible for the creation of modern civilization,[38] a trend conspicuously bypassed by the Anabaptists and their descendants.

Backsliding and Anfechtung. The Anabaptists tried to live as purely as a regenerated man may live, but they never

claimed to be without sin.[39] They knew that life is a perpetual struggle against all kinds of temptations and *Anfechtun-
gen*, and rare are the leaders who achieved the ultimate
goal of genuine *imitatio Christi*. Even during the most inspired
beginnings, between 1525 and 1530, when the spiritual power
of the movement was strongest, they knew only too well that
they could not achieve a complete victory over sin or, better,
a complete freedom from self-will. Backsliding to the "old
Adam" was an ever-present possibility, and the need for
watchful brethren or elders who would admonish or practice
mutual discipline (according to Matthew 18) was indisputable.
It was an act of brotherly love to admonish, to warn, or if
need be even to ban a brother who strayed too far from the
path of faithful discipleship. Often they even felt that the
harder the outward life, with prison and privations of all
kinds, the less the temptation for backsliding; and vice versa,
the softer the outward life and the more persecution receded
and gave way to a comfortable middle-class existence (as for
instance in the Netherlands after 1580), the greater the
likelihood of slackening and greater conformity to the surrounding world.[40]

Quite revealing in this context is what Hans Hut, one of
the earliest inspired apostles of the new faith in South Germany, had to say concerning sin and sinning. In his
tract, *Ein christlicher Unterricht* (1527), he writes:

> In this church (*Gemeinde*) all the members are brought
> together who detest sin and who love righteousness. And
> even though such a person might on occasion sin and go
> wrong, it is still not done intentionally for sheer pleasure.
> For that reason he will not be condemned. For the Lord
> holds him in His hand and his sin will be forgiven and not
> counted against him as sin. Such a person already belongs
> to the kingdom of God and has Christ as his Lord.[41]

The theology here involved might be debatable, yet it reflects
very well the mood of the incipient movement. No testimonial
of this kind is known in later times, and most likely
would not have been acceptable to the brethren in general.

The Anabaptists never indulged in any defense of "antinomianism" as their theological opponents, especially Bullinger, charged.[42] Its claim that under the gospel dispensation the moral law is no longer obligatory for the believer was never promoted or even countenanced by any evangelical Anabaptist.[43] In fact it was occasionally denounced as the inherent weakness of the opposing camp which relied all too much on the unmerited grace of God. This is well illustrated by the well-known stanza by Ludwig Haetzer (1528) (in free translation):

Yes, says the world, there is no need
That I with Christ should suffer,
Since Christ did suffer death for me
I may just sin on his account,
He pays for me, this I believe,
And thus the point is settled.

O brethren mine, it's but a sham,
The devil has contrived it.[44]

Certainly, to the Anabaptists the question whether to obey or not to obey the moral law was never present. As people ready to follow Christ, they would not even consider any other way but that described in Scripture again and again. They knew (1 John 3:6) that "whosoever abideth in him sinneth not," or would at least attempt this way of life. The *Handbüchlein* of 1558 mentioned above defends the Anabaptist position briefly by affirming: "As long as the believer is fighting soldierlike in the faith of Christ, the glory of God is reflected in him,"[45] even though the struggle may never cease.

We have not been dealing here with the technicalities of ban and exclusion from the brotherhood (or the hoped-for repentance and readmission) — some of the most basic functions of the brotherhood-church. Rather, our intent has been to stress the idea that the Anabaptist vision of Christianity "was not regulated by the concept of sin,"[46] as contrasted to normative Protestantism. Furthermore, the Anabaptists never indulged in the easy thesis that a reborn man could no longer sin. In this regard their position on sin was quite original and unique, considering the mood of the sixteenth century. And it becomes obvious that in a framework of thought where sin is understood as a force which at least to a large extent can be overcome, the idea of salvation from the consequences of man's sinful nature likewise loses its preponderance or centrality — hence the difficulty in communication with the representatives of the official state churches who simply could not understand this vision.

(B) *Love, the Countervailing Force to Sin*

Love as a constitutive element of man created in the image of God (which image was never completely wiped out) represents in the Anabaptist anthropology a rather novel point. Love *(agape)*, central to the teachings of Christ and His apostles, did not assume a central function in the theology of Protestantism, except as defined by the limits inherent within the "ethics of the individual" (as a private person, not as a citizen of the state). With the Anabaptists the situation is of necessity different, inasmuch as the Christian life begins with the experience of regeneration, newness of life, and discipleship. Here love is constitutive to the anthropology of the Anabaptists and supplies the force by which sin can be fought. Here love is more than "ethics"; it is an actual part of the vision of man, existentially conceived.

Sebastian Franck, generally a reliable source for early Anabaptism, has this to report in his *Chronica* of 1531: "As far as one could see they taught nothing but love, faith and the cross. They broke bread with one another as evidence of unity and love. They helped each other faithfully with mutual aid, lending and giving, and they taught that all things should be held in common."[47]

The idea of love as a central principle in existential Christianity seems to have been envisioned right from the beginning of the Anabaptist movement. In a debate with the brethren in Zurich in 1525/26, Zwingli asked "whether a person

might not be a Christian secretly and privately." Felix
Mantz answered unhesitatingly with a loud "No! Because
Christian and brotherly love requires that everyone is bound
to show it to his brother in the open."[48]

Not long afterward Hans Denck wrote his most beautiful,
small, but weighty tract *Von der wahren Liebe* (earlv 1527),
which exerted a tremendous influence upon both South and
Central German Anabaptism and was echoed everywhere [49] By
emphasizing that the law of God was given to man in the form
of love, Denck claimed that this was then the only way to
bring the believer nearer to God's own love. "He who understands this love but teaches otherwise is a genuine anti-
christ. But he who does not understand it has not really
recognized the Lord Christ."[50] This tract is found in a great
many Hutterite codices of the sixteenth and seventeenth
centuries, proving its great popularity and approval by the
brethren.

Man, the Anabaptists claimed, is not only a sinner but
also a person capable of loving, as follows so clearly from the
two supreme laws taught by Christ: love of God and love of
the neighbor. Love means first and foremost brotherhood, the
caring for the neighbor, and subsequently also a sharing with
fellow believers, as Sebastian Franck so keenly observed. In
fact, brotherly love implies quite naturally the desire to
share with the brother not only joy and sorrow but also
worldly goods as far as it is practically possible. The idea of
community of goods was championed by numerous early Anabaptists long before the Hutterites actually established their
communal settlements. It was, for instance, frankly confessed by
Ambrosius Spittelmaier (a convert of Hans Hut) at his trial in
1527, and defended with unusual vigor, even though this
brother never had a chance to practice his convictions.[51] In a
major Hutterite tract this principle of community of goods
is elaborated on under the significant heading, "Concerning
True Surrender."[52] And about one century later, the Hutterite bishop Andreas Ehrenpreis wrote a remarkable *Sendbrief*
with the following subtitle: *Brüderliche Gemeinschaft, das
höchste Gebot der Liebe betreffend* (1650, printed 1652), which

contains the significant admission: "Where the love of Christ
is not able to accomplish as much towards one's neighbor as
to have fellowship with him also in temporal needs, there the
blood of Christ cannot cleanse from sin."[53] — a radical
statement, which was most likely not readily accepted by all
Anabaptists.

Understandably, quotations from Anabaptist sources for
this basic vision of love[54] are not as numerous and many-
sided as they are for the topic of sin. Still, the mere fact
of closely knit Anabaptist brotherhoods reminiscent of the brotherhood-churches of the early Christians is a strong indication
of the dynamics of this vision. One does not theologize about
it; one simply lives it. The best illustration as far as literary
evidence is concerned may be found in the Anabaptists'
unique understanding of the Lord's Supper, interpreted as a
fellowship meal.[55]

Moving testimonials of the existential concreteness of
brotherly love are the innumerable epistles of the Anabaptists
which often literally overflow with loving concern for the
brother. Thus, for instance, in his fine epistle of 1528 to the
congregation of Rattenberg, Wolfgang Brandhuber says:

> If we want to be one with Christ we also have to be one
> with his will, and that means that we love him. If we love
> him then we will also keep his words. For if there should be
> love it must be in the heart. True Christianity knows noth-
> ing but love. It needs no law but fulfills the law out of sheer
> love, leaves everything, seeks whom it loves, and the more it
> loves, the more it desires to love and is glad that it can
> love. O brethren, where there is no love . . . what does it
> matter if one knows much, talks and teaches much, and
> yet does not love?[56]

The idea of love surfaces still stronger in the epistles of
Jacob Hutter, where the term "heart" occurs time and again.
Hutter often speaks of and to his "beloved children," his
brethren "whom I have carried in my heart," and so on.[57] But
this inner attitude is much more than mere emotionalism and
a far cry from pietistic sentimentality.[58] As an illustration we

quote Jeronymus Käls, the Anabaptist schoolteacher from Tyrol, martyred at Vienna in 1536. At his trial he had this to say to his persecutors:

> We wish and desire only good for all men and do not intend to hurt anybody, neither the pope nor monk and parson, neither emperor nor king, in fact no creature. Our conscience is free, pure and unburdened that we have no evil intentions or vengeance in our hearts. For this we are ready to suffer gladly and with great patience whatever God allows you to do with us.[59]

Thus spoke a man facing the stake, making true his baptismal pledge that it be "a covenant of a good conscience with God" (1 Peter 3:21). Over and over again we meet this mood at the most horrible trials: no hatred, but only love and forgiveness.

"It is impossible," wrote the Philippite brother Hans Haffner around 1534 in his outstanding tract, *Von einem wahrhaften Ritter Christi*, "that those who truly have faith which is given to them through Christ should not love God in return, yea, not only God but also their neighbors."[60] And Peter Walpot wrote in 1547: "Love does not seek its own, therefore it seeks indeed only to have fellowship. For love is a bond of perfection. Where it dwells it does not work a partial, but a complete and entire community."[61]

Love is also the preferred theme in Anabaptist hymnody as a recent student of it so pointedly observed: "Love is treated in Anabaptist hymnody more frequently than any other single belief."[62] Michael Schneider sings in the dungeon of Passau in 1535/36 as follows (in free translation):

> The man who does not follow Christ,
> Christ has not saved with his blood
> Nor forgiven his sins . . .[63]

This expresses an idea almost identical with Ehrenpreis' statement of 1650, quoted above.

Love, consequently, is part and parcel of salvation. For all these brethren, salvation was not possible without man's active response to the call of Christ, which in turn, resulted in love.[64] Hänsel Schmidt sang in the prison of Aachen in Germany, while waiting for his execution (1558):

> Love is recognized through word, life, and deed;
> For the Spirit of God dwells in the man
> who gives himself utterly to God. (Stanza 12)
> . . . .
> Dear brothers and sisters — children of God, pure in heart;
> Let us continually strive to love. (Stanza 26)[65]

The *Ausbund*, Hymn 124, dealing with true *Nachfolge*, has these lines:

> But foremost, apply love,
> Through which we overcome, while on this life's course;
> It is the bond of perfection, Love is God Himself,
> It remains in eternity.[66]

As to literary form, it is perhaps not great poetry, but it is a most genuine expression of the Anabaptist frame of mind even when facing brutal execution at the stake.

All these hymns were, of course, not composed with a theological issue in mind, but they truly reflect the mood seen throughout Anabaptist history. Man is not only and not primarily a sinner deserving eternal punishment save for the unmerited grace he receives through faith. The Anabaptists would rather say: As man receives grace a new life arises in his heart and makes him ready to be a follower of Christ, and as such to be a lover of his neighbor and a brother to his fellow believer. By this he also conquers, at least to a certain extent, the sinful urge in his soul. Anthropology thus assumes a new aspect and answers the problem of human existence in the affirmative.

Footnotes to "Anthropology"

1. See Torsten Bergsten, *Balthasar Hubmaier, seine Stellung zu Reformation und Täufertum*, 1961, Chapter Nine: "Nachwirkungen von Hubmaiers Lebenswerk in der Zeit der Reformation und Gegenreformation," 482-502.

2. English translation in George H. Williams, *Spiritual and Anabaptist Writers* (Library of Christian Classics, XXV), 1957, 114-135, with a fine introduction.

3. In our day Nikolay Berdyaev, the outstanding Russian philosopher, also espoused such a trichotomic anthropology throughout his numerous works.

4. Bergsten, *op. cit.*, 443.

5. Balthasar Hubmaier, *Schriften*, ed., Torsten Bergsten and G. Westin, 1962, 390, 392.

6. *Ibid.*, 386.

7. *Ibid.*, 322. The German sentence runs as follows: "Die Bildung [Bild] Gottes ist je noch nicht gar in uns ausgewischt."

8. Balthasar Hubmaier, "Von der christlichen Taufe der Gläubigen," (1525) in *Schriften*, 120: "Dass wir uns aber berühmen sollten, als mögen wir nach der Tauff nimmer sünden, geschicht uns daran unrecht, denn wir wissend, dass wir vor und nach [der Taufe] arme und elende sünder seyend." This is perhaps Hubmaier's most outstanding tract.

9. See Frank Wray, "Free Will with the Anabaptists," *ME*, II, 367-369.

10. Hubmaier, *op. cit.*, 387, referring to Psalm 119:7.

11. Pilgram Marpeck, *Verantwortung*, ed., Johann Loserth (Vienna, 1929), 196 ff.

12. As Torsten Bergsten made clear in his "Notes" to *Das andere Büchlein von der Freiwilligkeit des Menschen*, 1527, in Hubmaier, *Schriften*, 398 f. See also Thor Hall, "Possibilities of Erasmian Influence on Denck and Hubmaier in Their Views on the Freedom of Will," *MQR*, XXXV (1961), 149-170.

13. Leonhard Schiemer, under obvious influence of Hubmaier's teachings, developed the doctrine of a threefold grace (*Von dreierlei Gnade*, 1527). See below.

14. See the excellent article, "Love," by Don. Smucker|in *ME*, III, 404, |405.

15. Lydia Müller, *Glaubenszeugnisse* (1938), 233: "Ein ander Sendbrief über die Erbsünde," by Ulrich Stadler, 1536.

16. *Ibid.*

17. The Apostle Paul never overstressed the hopelessness of man due to the fall of Adam, for he knew only too well the possibility of a renewal of the heart.

18. As to the Fourth Book of Esdras, see *ME*, II, 283, with literature.

19. Sebastian Franck, *Chronica, Zeytbuch und Geschychtsbibel* (first ed., 1531), 447. See also the article "Chronica" in *ME*, I, 587-589.

20. Robert Friedmann, "Claus Felbinger's Confession of 1560," *MQR*, XXIX (1955), 158.

21. Robert Friedmann, "Peter Riedemann on Original Sin and the Way of Redemption," *MQR*, XXVI (1952), 210 ff. See also Friedmann, "Original Sin," *ME*, IV, 79-82.:

22. Hans Georg Fischer, *Jakob Huter* (1956), "Briefe," VI, 47.

23. See Friedmann, "Taufreden," *ME*, IV, 686, 687. These *Taufreden* (late sixteenth century) are at present available only in Hutterite codices. Their publication is planned for volume III of the *Glaubenszeugnisse oberdeutscher Taufgesinnter*.

24. See Friedmann, "Handbüchlein," *ME*, II, 645, 646, with bibliography.

25. See Friedmann, "Bedenken," *ME*, I, 261.

26. W. Wiswedel, "The Anabaptists Answer Melanchthon," *MQR*, XXIX (1955), 217, 218.

27. Lydia Müller, *Glaubenszeugnisse*, 217, 232.

28. *Ibid.*, 228.

29. John Umble, "An Amish Minister's Manual," *MQR*, XV (1941), 101. Here we read that the Amish are still using the Book of Tobit as a fitting text for wedding sermons.

30. "The external eating" for "der äussere Anbiss"; and "if it had not been accompanied by an inner acceptance at heart" for "wenn die innerliche Annahme ausblieben wäre." Manfred Krebs, ed., *Täuferakten, Baden-Pfalz* (1951), 114. See also M. Krebs and H. G. Rott, *Täuferakten, Elsass*, I (1959), 105; and Christian Hege, *Täufer in der Kurpfalz* (1908), 34-37. Martin Bucer's answer is in *Täuferakten, Elsass I*, 105 ff. It was Hans Hut who first used the term "verwilligen" for the same idea. (See L. Müller, *Glaubenszeugnisse*, 20 and *passim*.)

31. Emil Egli, *Die Züricher Wiedertäufer* (1878), No. 692. Also von Muralt-Schmidt, *Quellen zur Geschichte der Täufer in der Schweiz*, Vol. I (Zürich, 1951), No. 200.

32. Peter Rideman, *Account of Our Religion* (Eng. ed. 1950), 56.

33. See Friedmann, "Gelassenheit," *ME*, II, 448,449; Hans J. Hillerbrand, "Andreas Bodenstein of Carlstadt, Prodigal Reformer," *Church History* (1966), 379-398, pointed to the fact that *Gelassenheit* is also a central idea in the writings of Carlstadt.

34. What Max Weber had called "innerworldly asceticism" is still being practiced by the Hutterites and Amish of today.

35. By this the Hutterite author meant that any pure and saintly life would eventually provoke persecution and suffering, since the world simply cannot countenance such nonconformity.

36. The *Taufreden* are still in use today among the Hutterites for their candidates of baptism. Since about 1600 they have remained practically unchanged. The earliest ones extant are of 1584 and 1599.

37. Reinhold Niebuhr, *Nature and Destiny of Man* (1941).

38. The literature on this topic is very large. Besides Reinhold Niebuhr's work the most original treatment is by Robert Payne (London), *Hubris, a Study of Pride* (1960), Harper's Torchbook No. 1031. R. W. Emerson's essay on "Self-Reliance" falls in the same category.

39. As David Joris, for instance, taught, or the Pietists of the eighteenth century.

40. See the very interesting Introduction to the old Swiss Mennonite book *Güldene Aepffel in Silbern Schalen* (1702), which runs as follows: "It is true that external peace makes the number of those who profess Christian faith to increase. But it is also true that at such times of ease for the flesh Satan insinuates to man all sorts of evil suggestions, and he is wont to approach the believer very subtly. So depraved is human nature that it cannot endure good days of ease. The soul then becomes corrupt as it becomes fond of the world. Therefore, to awaken people to a living faith which works by love, writings of our forefathers have been collected. May they lead the hearts of the readers to the obedience of the truth." See Friedmann, *Mennonite Piety* (1949), 104, 159.

41. Müller, *Glaubenszeugnisse*, 36.

42. Williams, *The Radical Reformation* (1962), 202, 203, where Bullinger's *Von dem unverschämpten fräfel, ergerlichen verwyrren und unwarhafften leeren der selbsgesandten Wiedertäuffern* (Zürich, 1531) is discussed. Bullinger denounces the (Swiss) Anabaptists for antinomian behavior, and his thesis soon became a generally accepted slander against all nonconformists.

43. The Hutterite *Chronicle* mentions, for the year 1576, one such rather foolish case where a brother in Moravia claimed that through faith he was not only relieved of the burden of his actual sins but even of the further inclination to sin. He was first admonished by the elders to desist from such teachings, and when this did not bring any change of mind, he was finally excommunicated. See A. J. F. Zieglschmid, ed. *Die älteste Chronik* (1943), 478.

44. "Ei, spricht die Welt, es ist ohn Not / Dass ich mit Christo leide . . *Lieder der Hutterischen Brüder* (Scottdale, Pa., 1914), 29; *MQR*, XXVIII (1954), 34.

45. Wiswedel, "The Anabaptists Answer Melanchthon," *MQR*, XXIX (1955), 219, 220.

46. A. Orley Swartzentruber, "The Piety and Theology of the Anabaptist Martyrs

in van Braght's *Martyrs Mirror,*" *MQR*, XXVIII (1954), 5 ff., 128 ff. The entire study
is most excellent and by far the profoundest on our subject.
47. Sebastian Franck, *Chronica*, fol. 444v.
48. Von Muralt and W. Schmidt, *Quellen*, 127.
49. John Oyer, "Anabaptism in Central Germany," *MQR*, XXXV (1961), 36.
50. Walter Fellmann, ed., *Hans Denck, Schriften*, II (1956), 85.
51. Herbert Klassen, "Ambrosius Spittelmayer," *MQR*, XXXII (1958), 259.
52. "Von der waren Gelassenheit und der christlichen Gemeinschaft der Güter"
(Concerning True Surrender and Christian Community of Goods), ed. by R. Friedmann,
MQR, XXXI (1957), 25 ff.
53. Andreas Ehrenpreis, *Sendbrief* (reprint, 1920), 49.
54. In his *Anabaptist Vision* (1944, many reprints), Harold S. Bender calls this
element of love "ethics of love," a Greek term that does not quite fit this Christian
existential situation. Love is not an element of ethics (behavior) but of man's spiritual
constitution.
55. See Friedmann, "Lord's Supper," *ME*, III, 394, 395. This point will be discussed
in greater detail in the chapter on ecclesiology below.
56. Müller, *Glaubenszeugnisse*, 142.
57. See Friedmann, "Jacob Hutter's Last Epistle to the Church in Moravia, 1535,"
MQR, XXXIV (1960), 41-47.
58. May I be permitted to add here a personal note of some relevance. It was this
observation of emotional stress which long ago aroused in me the idea to study the in-
terrelationship between Anabaptism and Pietism, the result of which is my book, *Mennonite Piety*, 1949. It is true that occasionally, epistles of the Hutterites assume a
quasi-pietistic flavor through this strong emphasis upon love and the "heart," but a
closer look reveals basic differences. The true proto-Pietist of the sixteenth century
was Caspar Schwenckfeld and not Jacob Hutter or Brandhuber.
59. Müller, *Glaubenszeugnisse*, 210.
60. Friedmann, "Concerning the True Soldier of Christ, a Hitherto Unknown Tract
of the Philippite Brethren," *MQR*, V (1931), 93.
61. *Die älteste Chronik der Hutterischen Brüder*, ed., A. J. F. Zieglschmid (1943),
294.
62. Rosella Reimer Duerksen, "Doctrinal Implications in Sixteenth Century Anabaptist Hymnody," *MQR*, XXXV (1961), 40.
63. "Wer aber ihm nit folgen thut / Den hat auch nit erlöst sein Blut, /Sein
Sünden auch nit vergeben . . ." *Ausbund* (any edition), Hymn No. 82, st. 4.
64. Rudolf Wolkan, in his *Lieder der Wiedertäufer* (1903), repeatedly observed this
unique emphasis upon love.
65. *Lieder der Hutterischen Brüder* (1914), 564-567.
66. Rosella Reimer Duerksen, *op. cit.*, 41.

❮

Soteriology:
Salvation - Justification - Grace

In the light of the preceding discussion it should not be surprising that "soteriology," traditionally the very nucleus of all theology, is not and cannot be a major theme in Anabaptist thought. The concern as to "how to escape eternal damnation," or in Luther's terms, "how to find a gracious God," was certainly not a major concern of the Anabaptists. As has been said, they did not start with the crushing awareness of being lost sinners but began rather with the glorious experience of regeneration or spiritual rebirth. This signifies basically a positive experience of God's grace which subsequently leads to a rather different chain of insights. Granted, it was rather uncommon, this experience which so overwhelmed seekers that they spontaneously joined the flock of Anabaptist disciples wherever they found them.[1] These early Anabaptists were not particularly bothered by guilt feelings; they desired to walk in the footsteps of the Master, "in love and cross," as Sebastian Franck described them. Therefore, the question of "salvation" naturally dropped into the background and was dealt with only casually.

A personal experience may serve to dramatize this situation and make the genius of Anabaptism come more alive. Several years ago, after a conference in South Dakota, a number of ministers decided to visit a nearby Hutterite Bruderhof, the oldest one in the United States, and I was invited to join this group. We were cordially received and shown around and then the elders were ready to discuss their way of life. One of the first questions the ministers asked was this: "What do you people teach regarding salvation?" Thereupon the very intelligent brother, who had very likely not anticipated this question, paused a moment and then said quietly but with great assurance: "If we live in obedience to God's commandments, we are certain of being in God's gracious hands; we do not worry further about our salvation. Rather, we try to walk the narrow path in the fear of the Lord. We fight sin and practice brotherly love. How then can redemption be lacking?" This reply was as simple as it was authentic. Now it was the ministers, trained in conventional theology, who were surprised and even a bit shocked. They had not anticipated such an answer.

One may rashly judge that such teachings smack of *Werkgerechtigkeit* (meritorious acts). But that would be a serious misinterpretation of such a statement as the one above, true to an ancient tradition. As early as 1541 Peter Riedemann, one of the great lights of early Hutterianism, vigorously denied this reproach in his great *Rechenschaft* as follows:

> Many say of us that we seek to be good [fromb] through our own works. To this we say "No," for we know that our work, in so far as it is *our* work, is naught but sin and unrighteousness; but insofar as it is of Christ and done by *Christ in us*, so far is it truth.[2]

Peter Walpot, in his *Great Article Book* of 1577, wrote in a similar vein, while discussing the story of the rich young man in Matthew 19: "To give to the poor should not be understood in such a way as if being poor could save the young man. That he follows Christ in his words and commands: that alone is what saves him."[3] This expresses quite generally the idea held by most Anabaptists. It is living in "childlike obedience" without any thought of "working" for salvation or gaining merits by work that was meant by the Anabaptists of four centuries ago, as well as the Hutterite brothers in South Dakota today.

Thus the subject of soteriology does not really occupy the center of Anabaptist thought but receives its relevance primarily against the background of the tension between normative Protestantism and Anabaptism. It was only natural that the soteriological question should arise frequently in debates and court trials, and the brethren had to clarify their stand concerning salvation, justification, and atonement. But in principle the soteriological problems are furthest from the type of existential Christianity which we have claimed to be the center of Anabaptism. In a sense, then, we meet here truly the acid test of our entire thesis concerning Anabaptist theology.

Within the topic of soteriology, we distinguish three subjects: (a) the idea of redemption proper and how it is achieved; (b) the idea of justification, or its possible alternative; and (c) the idea of grace within the Anabaptist understanding of the divine-human encounter.

(A)

Concerning Redemption and How It Is Being Achieved

In a preceding chapter we noted how Andreas Ehrenpreis linked redemption to the love which includes a sharing in both spiritual and temporal needs. Michael Schneider understood redemption in relationship to following Christ. And an old Hutterite bishop in Canada said to me a few years ago: "It is only through communal living (*Gemeinschaft*) that the blood of Christ may cleanse sinful man. Christ cannot help us unless we follow him all the way without reservation."[4]

These are weighty, though rather unorthodox theologoumena, and worthy of further analysis. A schematic comparison of Catholic, Protestant, and Anabaptist ideas on how to approach God to find redemption is in order: In Catholicism the believer is offered, as the only effective way to God and salvation, an intermediary, the institutional church with its reservoir of divine grace, and with its ordained priests who dispense the sacraments. In Protestantism this intermediary was radically done away with. Every individual believer stands in direct, unmediated relationship to his God, seeking and finding redemption by faith to the extent that he is able to have such a redeeming faith. In Anabaptism, finally, the answer is a combination of a vertical with a horizontal relationship. Here the thesis is accepted that *man cannot come to God except together with his brother.* In other words, the brother, the neighbor, constitutes an essential element of one's personal redemption. For the disciple there is no such thing as an isolated Christian in his lonely cell. To him brotherhood is not merely an ethical adjunct to Christian theological thinking but an integral condition for any genuine restoration of God's image in man (which after all is the deepest meaning of redemption).

A simple graph may illustrate the relationship between God and man for these three major theological positions:

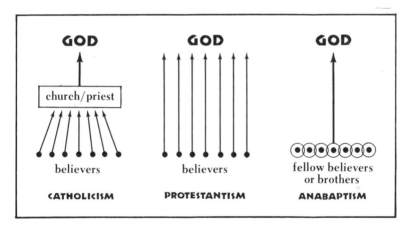

This Anabaptist vision of man's way to God seems to be an acceptable understanding of the teaching of the Gospels and a profound justification for the strong fellowship ties among the Anabaptist brotherhood-churches.

It has always been claimed that the brotherhood-church (*Gemeinde*) served a central function within Anabaptism. The reason for this was apparently that only in the *Gemeinde* can the believer apply Christian love in action. Only here can the believer realize his convictions that he cannot come to God in good conscience except with his brother. Whether such fellowship should go as far as including community of goods (as with the Hutterites) or only as far as caring for needy brethren was never fully agreed upon, even though ideally full community of goods was recognized as·a desirable goal by many early Anabaptists. The intimate fellowship, the concern for the brethren and their needs, was actually present everywhere, in stark contrast to the established state churches, both Catholic and Protestant. In fact, the *Gemeinde* always had some traits which were understood by the brethren as a "foretaste of the kingdom of God," such as the living together in peace and mutual exhortation, or the sharing of both spiritual and material things.

It must be granted, however, that in the earliest period, which was certainly the most inspired period of Anabaptism, *Gemeinden* were hardly in existence, at least not. in any organized form, due to harsh persecutions. Only in Moravia could such churchlike brotherhoods develop, with their corresponding theological interpretation. Elsewhere we find scattered small groups which might convene now and then at night in forest glens or remote cottages or mills to celebrate a simple Lord's Supper in love-feast fashion. Thus the question of redemption and salvation (the two terms fairly interchangeable) had to be answered independently of the existence of a concrete church body. It is therefore fitting to begin our discussion with the study of the early Anabaptist understanding of the issue of salvation regardless of any church organization.

The earliest "Anabaptist" document in existence is Conrad Grebel's epistle to Thomas Müntzer, dated September 5, 1524, several months before the first adult baptism had taken place in January 1525, and before any church had been formed. Grebel writes to Müntzer:

> Faith must have fruits, otherwise it is a false or hypocritical faith. If one separates oneself from sin, one may be sure of salvation. Baptism signifies that a man is dead, or ought to be dead, to sin and is *walking in the newness of life* and spirit. Such a one shall certainly be saved if, according to this idea, through inner baptism he lives his faith.[5]

In other words, salvation is not simply the certitude of being saved from damnation (which is only a reassuring idea of feeling), but a "walking in newness of life"; or in another formulation, "the transformation into a new creature in whom Christ is increasingly being formed."[6]

Some of the profoundest statements concerning salvation come from this earliest period of Anabaptism, a time when it was not yet completely separated from a sort of biblical spiritualism. One of the (unpublished) tracts of Hans Schlaffer (martyred in 1528) contains the revealing confession: "And even if Christ had died a hundredfold it would be of no avail to me unless the spiritual Christ would be preached as well."[7] And further: "He who goes into hell with Christ and *in* Christ, will also be led out of hell again *with* Christ."[8] Generally speaking Schlaffer teaches, in good Pauline fashion, "to be crucified with Christ, to be buried with him and to be resurrected with him" (Romans 6:3-5; Colossians 2:12). But he formulated his profoundest insight in the doctrine of the *Tiefe Christi*, a doctrine similar to the idea of *kenosis* in Philippians 2:7, the idea of the utter humiliation of Christ Himself.[9] ("Man muss durch diese Tiefe hindurchgehen, wenn man durch Christus erlöst werden will.") This "depth," he says, is "the lowliness and resignation into which everyone is led, and it is called hell. This depth is the sign of Jonah (Matthew 12:39). Into this depth all men have to go who long to be saved *in* Christ." Pilgram Marpeck espoused almost the same idea, for instance, in his letter of February 1, 1547, to the brethren in Graubünden, Appenzell, and Alsace entitled "Von der Tiefe Christi."[10]

The Satisfaction of Christ. Two more related problems deserve our attention: the doctrine of the "Satisfaction of Christ," again strongly ideological, hence marginal to Anabaptist thinking; and the idea of suffering as a way of redemption — in other words the alternative of the "bitter" versus the "sweet" Savior, originating first with Thomas Müntzer but with a strong appeal also to the martyr-minded Anabaptists.

As for the idea of "satisfaction" (*Genugtuung*) of Christ
for our sins, Williams suggests that the idea of "ransoming"
man through the cross was definitely neglected by Anabaptists in favor of a more active sharing in the spiritual
process of redemption.[11] In the entire Anabaptist tract
literature we encounter only one tract: *Concerning the
Satisfaction of Christ*,[12] anonymous to be sure (but possibly
written by Sattler) and of a rather early date (before 1530).
Strictly speaking, this tract typically does not really discuss
the subject of "atonement" or the satisfaction of Christ. It
rather deals with the more existential question. *To whom
may the blessings of atonement apply?* Who is entitled
to claim that Christ "died for him," and what does it mean to
the believer that Christ, according to Paul, is "the reconciliation of the world"? To this the unknown author gives
the answer that the "satisfaction" is efficacious only for
those who, in faith, live the Christian life (meaning in self-
denial, good works, and cross-bearing), and who expose
themselves to suffering in the world. In brief, the faith
which may hope for salvation through atonement must be a
tested or tried faith. One passage states this clearly: "Paul
does not mean that a man can be saved without the works
of faith." And one page later the author says most outspokenly:

> He who does not [keep the commandments] and yet
> boasts of Christ as being his reconciliation is a liar, inas-
> much as he has never known Christ. . . . How then did
> Christ make satisfaction ("do enough") for our sins?
> Answer: [He did enough] not only for ours, but also
> for the sins of the whole world . . . insofar as they believe
> on Him and follow Him according to the demands of
> faith. . . . *Repentance is not apart from works, yea not
> apart from love.* . . . Only such an anointed faith . . . is
> reckoned for righteousness.[13]

That such teachings are not isolated speculations can
fortunately be demonstrated. Around the same time that this
tract was written, the Palatine Anabaptist Jakob Kautz defended almost exactly the same ideas, most likely independent-

ly of the above tract. As stated in the previous chapter, Kautz challenged the Protestant clergy of the city of Worms with his "Seven Theses" on June 13, 1527. Thesis Six runs as follows:

Jesus Christ of Nazareth did not suffer for us and has not satisfied [for our sins] in any other way but this: that we have to stand in his footsteps and have to walk the way which he had blazed for us first, and that we obey the commandments of the Father and the Son, everyone according to his measure. He who speaks differently of Christ makes an idol of Christ.[14]

The Lutheran clergy, of course, had little sympathy for this kind of teaching; to them it was outright heretical. Not long thereafter Martin Bucer of Strassburg elaborately answered this thesis and unfortunately acted very uncharitably toward Kautz when the latter, sick and broken, asked for asylum. We do not know how many Anabaptists shared Kautz's theology but that it was sound "early Anabaptist theology" can easily be adduced also from another case. A Thuringian brother testified at his trial in 1537: "The death of Christ has no validity for any person who does not imitate Christ in purity of life."[15]

Ambrosius Spittelmaier expressed the same idea in his Confession of Faith (1527); in fact, the more the sources become known to scholarship, the more we discover the great similarity of most Anabaptist enunciations, whether Swiss, South German, or Hutterite. "Without the cross [my suffering], God cannot save me in spite of all His power," said Leonhard Schiemer in his prison cell at Rattenberg, Tyrol, in 1527/28.[16] It is his only justification for being in jail and facing death, expressing the deep Anabaptist belief in the redemptive quality of the cross. Not the isolated event at Calvary alone, but the cross that every believer faces when consistently living a life of discipleship is what works toward salvation. The way of the cross, however, has also "opened for us the kingdom of heaven from which we had fallen because of Adam."[17]

The Bitter Versus the Sweet Christ. This brings us to
the last topic of this section, the hidden antithesis of the
"bitter Christ" versus the "sweet Christ," or as we could
also say in contemporary idiom: the antithesis of costly grace
versus cheap grace (Bonhoeffer). Johann Loserth called it
symbolically "the crown of thorns" versus "the halo of
glory."[18] It has a profound bearing on the issue here discussed. Thomas Müntzer's *Vom gedichteten Glauben* (1524) may
be considered the best representation of this idea: "He who
refuses the bitter Christ will eat his death with honey.
. . . For he who will not die with Christ cannot rise with
him either."[19] As man desires to become like Christ he
cannot help but meet his cross daily. Of course this peculiar Müntzerite teaching, the "theology of the cross," is
not precisely the same as the "theology of martyrdom"
among the Anabaptists who were thinking primarily in
terms of the "suffering church" as a whole. Nevertheless, the
antithesis, the "bitter" versus the "sweet" Christ, also fits
very well as a description of the Anabaptist philosophy of
life. "The world accepts Christ as a gift," wrote the Anabaptist Hans Haffner in 1534, "but it does not know him
as a suffering Christ (*leidenderweise*)."[20] Marpeck's conflict with Schwenckfeld seems to have had its roots at exactly this point; for Schwenckfeld was the passionate champion
of the "glorified Christ" while Marpeck taught the crucified
Redeemer.

Hans Hut even made this idea a universal one. Probably
borrowing from Müntzer, he espoused the idea of the "gospel
of all creatures," namely, that in all of God's creation, nothing
may be gained except through suffering: "*For man cannot find
redemption except through the cross and suffering.*"[21]

A word of caution: there is nothing mechanical or
automatic in this claim that salvation presupposes discipleship and often even martyrdom. It is the very secret of
spiritual life (as revealed in the experience of rebirth) that in
this kind of life different laws prevail from those in natural
life. Only on this new existential level does the insight
grow that redemption consists in a complete transvaluation

of conventional values, offering a mountaintop view where the perspective is changed and where the forces of love become as natural as the forces of self-assertion and competition on the lower level. That there is little room for an explicit theology in the scholastic sense of the word hardly requires further demonstration.

(B)

Concerning Justification or Its Substitute

"Justification [of the sinner] by faith" has become the very cornerstone of Protestant theology in general, even though in the epistles of Paul it does not loom as conspicuously as, for instance, in Luther's thought, who even added the little word "by faith *alone*" to make the emphasis still stronger. Thus it became the central Protestant doctrine, while its counterpart "sanctification" of the faithful in his daily life was neglected. The Anabaptists do not use the term *Rechtfertigung*, for to them the framework of Lutheran thinking was utterly foreign. This lack of reference has been noted many times by students of the Radical Reformation,[22] and they were quick to discover that one has to distinguish between *Gerechterklärung* (to pronounce as just) and *Gerechtmachung* (to make just or aright). The former is "forensic" in nature, as when a judge in court acquits a person, no matter whether guilty or not; he does it out of grace, or because of intercession by some powerful sponsor. The other is a change in the nature or quality of the person who first was, but no longer is — at least in intention — a sinner.

The distinction applies not only to the theology of the Anabaptists; even outspoken Lutherans like Dietrich Bonhoeffer would agree with it. In his classic *Cost of Discipleship* Bonhoeffer arrives at a very significant clarification in this regard. What he calls "cheap grace" would teach "justification *in sin*," that is, acquittal, even while man actually remains an unregenerate sinner. Luther's advice to Melanchthon already quoted earlier, *pecca fortiter* ("sin boldly . . . but believe and rejoice in Christ more boldly still"),[23] would lend an argument in this direction (even though Bonhoeffer defends Luther on this score).[24] What Bonhoeffer calls "costly grace" would teach "justification *out of sin*" or "from sin," which means actually such a spiritual change in man that he no longer wants to sin, indeed, that he wants to resist and overcome sin from now on.[25]

For the Anabaptists, of these two terms only that which is signified by *Gerechtmachung* is acceptable. Much more frequently, however, we find in Anabaptist texts the term *Fromm-Machung*,[26] the bringing of man into the right or proper relationship to God that makes him a genuine follower of Christ.[27] Such an interpretation of justification may be called existential rather than theological; it does not mean merely an acquittal in court but an actual change in man's nature.[28]

The first to use the term *Fromm-Machung* was apparently Balthasar Hubmaier. In his tract *Von der christlichen Taufe der Gläubigen*, the "Taufbüchlein" of 1525, the last chapter is entitled "Von der ordnung einer christlichen fromb-machung,"[29] where he says that Christ is "our physician who came into this world to make sinners righteous and God-fearing (*fromb*)"; a few lines later he speaks of *Gesund-Machung* (making healthy). And again a page later we read that the Spirit of God works in the believers and makes them "*fromb, gerecht und geystlich.*" In his *Christliche Lehrtafel* (1526) he pens the remarkable admission: "And although faith alone makes God-fearing (*fromb*), it alone does not save man."[30] Hubmaier here adds weight to the points made in the preceding chapter.

One year later Hans Hut, in his *Vom Geheimnis der Taufe* (1527), wrote a great deal about man's response to God's call, understanding this response as acceptance (*Verwilligung*) of the divine covenant, or even perhaps as a pledge to the obedience to Christ. "No creature," he writes, "is able to justify himself as regards salvation. But if man is to be justified by God he must prepare himself that God may accomplish his work in him. . . . . Hence the water of tribulation[31] is the proper essence of baptism by which man may become lost in the death of Christ."[32] *Gerechtmachung* consequently means "participation in the suffering of Christ," which obviously is a far cry from the traditional forensic meaning of "justification by faith alone."

Inasmuch as Hut was truly an apostle of South German Anabaptism, his teachings deserve our greatest attention, justifying more quotations and references: "Man," he says,[33] "is justified and cleansed only under the cross," which to Hut is simply another term (cross) for a "tested or tried" faith. Accordingly, "The whole world fears righteousness like the devil and would gladly pay for it with a spurious faith"|(*erdichteter Glauben*, a term borrowed from Thomas Müntzer). Obviously the terms righteousness and justification here assume a new meaning and are not really pertinent to a theological analysis.[34]

The next witness, a most reliable one, is Peter Riedemann, who in his *Rechenschaft* (1541), in the chapter "We Believe in Jesus Christ,"[35] first criticizes the Lutherans who say that Christ is their righteousness and goodness (*frombkeit*) but continue to live in abomination.[36] And then he writes: "But we confess Christ to be our righteousness and goodness (John 15:1-10) because he himself works in us the righteousness and goodness through which we become loved of God. . . . For we have no goodness apart from that which he alone works in us (Philippians 3:8-14)." In his chapter, "Man Is Grafted into Christ," we read most succinctly: "We teach further that Christ came into the world *to make sinners blessed*" (free rendering of 1 Timothy 1:15).

A final clarification may be derived from a new source not used thus far, Leupold Scharnschlager's epistle to the brethren in Alsace, "Concerning True Faith and Salvation in Christ," written between 1545 and 1550:[37] "I teach you the righteousness of God (*Gerechtigkeit vor Gott*) which comes through faith in Jesus Christ to all and upon all who truly believe. And we are made *fromm* (God-fearing or right) without any merit of our own, only by His grace through the salvation of

Christ." Then he quotes Romans 5:1 and comments:

> Here you find it perfectly clear that like life eternal also the fear of God (*Frommigkeit*) and righteousness come to man by faith alone. For that reason those who perform external work should watch that such a faith (which is no work of man but a gift of God) is built up and well planted.

The change of tone here, when compared with the testimonials of twenty years earlier, is striking — no reference to cross and martyrdom; and a greater convergence toward Lutheran theology. The Marpeck brotherhood, to which Scharnschlager belonged, was certainly set apart somewhat from that of a Grebel, Hut, Schiemer, or Hutter. Harold S. Bender was not wrong when he claimed that theologically the Marpeck circle stood halfway between the Swiss Brethren and the Lutherans.[38]

Hans Georg Fischer, a Lutheran minister in Vienna, wrote a stimulating essay on "Lutheranism and the Vindication of the Anabaptist Way."[39] In it he laments, among other points, that Lutheranism with its overemphasis on justification completely neglects a stress on its counterpart, sanctification, although justification without sanctification is really an incomplete theological doctrine. "What matters at this point," he says,[40] "is the understanding that the principle *sola gratia* must not be restricted to the idea of justification of man *as a sinner*. It likewise applies to the idea of sanctification of man *as a follower of Christ*." And somewhat later he makes it even more definite: "Christ works in a twofold way: as the Christ *for* us He makes justification available to man. And as the Christ *in* us He leads man to sanctification." Sanctification, therefore, is the essential complement to justification. The Pietists two centuries after both Luther and the Anabaptists, swinging to the other extreme, made sanctification their exclusive concern, and they developed a real tactic toward such an achievement. Strangely enough, however, the term *Heiligung* hardly ever appears in Anabaptist writings, even though it is implied in terms such as *Fromm-Machung*, following Christ, obedience, and similar expressions. The full commitment to discipleship and the correlated idea of being cleansed through suffering is indeed an element in Anabaptist thought. This Lutheran minister has made a valuable contribution in calling the attention of students of Anabaptism to this important complement inherent in Anabaptist theological thought.

(C)
Concerning Grace Within the Anabaptist Understanding of the Divine-Human Encounter

Although grace is a basic biblical term used throughout the Scriptures and well known to the Anabaptists, neither the *Mennonite Encyclopedia* nor the *Mennonitisches Lexikon* has an article on it. Until recently practically no one has given any attention to the idea of grace in Anabaptist thought. How can this be explained? One reason may be the overstressed view of grace within Protestantism, understood as the marvelous force which alone redeems the sinner in spite of all his shortcomings. Thus the feeling could arise that Anabaptists (whose basic vision was so strongly oriented toward man's active response to God's call) simply paid no further theological attention to the role of grace in the divine arrangement of man's salvation. The accent was a different one. And Hans G. Fischer was right in saying that with Anabaptists *"the way of discipleship has precedence over the concern for salvation."*[41] A forensic view of grace, in which the sinner is forgiven and undeservedly justified, is simply unacceptable to the existential faith of the Anabaptists. But by no means does it imply that for such a reason the biblical idea of grace has no place in the outlook of a committed Christian.

Fortunately, in recent years several scholars have focused their attention in this direction and thus have helped toward a better understanding of the Anabaptist frame of mind.[42] Grace is a term rarely found in the four Gospels,[43] though it occurs in all later books of the New Testament. That may be one reason why the Anabaptists, who preferably read the

Gospels, were less interested in this idea than one might have expected. Oosterbaan brilliantly analyzes the meaning of the term as used by the different Christian bodies. In Catholicism, he claims that grace is an objective force, more correctly a substance (the church being a reservoir of grace), which is dispensed by the sacraments. In Protestantism grace means simply a "favor," like the grace of a sovereign. It signifies forgiving of sins or "the mercy which is promised for Christ's sake." As such it belongs to soteriological theology: it is the well-disposed favor of God toward the understanding sinner. It is "justifying grace."[44]

Regarding the Anabaptists, Oosterbaan observes that there always has been much misunderstanding in the churches of the Reformation regarding Anabaptist theology. These churches took a defensive attitude and were intent upon discovering heresy in their opponents. While the Council of Trent (1545-63) was an "abstract" negation of the Reformation, the Anabaptist movement in turn may be called a "concrete" negation intent on correcting certain extremes and above all everything that was not scriptural, thereby completing the Reformation proper. Grace with the Anabaptists is *not a soteriological term* (Oosterbaan claims) pointing to the favor and readiness of God to forgive. It rather signifies the *creative love* which is the very essence of God Almighty. God's grace then does not begin for the Dutch Mennonites as the reconciliation and forgiveness of sin, but at creation. "The human race is created by Jesus Christ out of grace." Because *grace is prior to sin*, it is also granted to infants before they come of age. This view of grace as the term for God's free and sovereign creative love is, according to Oosterbaan, the internal foundation for typically Anabaptist views of faith. It is, for instance, reflected in true repentance and the new life. In this sense the author claims that Anabaptist theology (at least with the Dutch Mennonites) bears clearly the character of a "theology of grace."[45]

By way of critique we ask whether such a theology perhaps could not be still better called a "theology of creative love." Oosterbaan's approach is also somewhat different from

ours in that the existential and experiential aspect, starting with
the new birth, was not essential in his analysis.

Alvin Beachy's study likewise starts from an approach different from both Oosterbaan's and ours. Beachy distinguishes
between a "forensic view of grace" (corresponding to the
idea of forensic justification) and an "ontological understanding"
of it, that is, its understanding as an act of God which brings
about an "ontological change" in the believer.[46] The reborn
man knows himself to be a "child of grace," a point which hits
well the central concern of our discussion. Balthasar Hubmaier,
in his fundamental tract *Von der Freiheit des Willens* (1527),
distinguishes between two types of grace: the freedom of Adam
before the Fall (actually unknown to us), and a new grace
which restored man to health. The restored "soul" together
with the unfallen "spirit" of man constitute the new man
who may or may not avail himself of the saving grace of
Christ. Unfortunately, Hubmaier does not develop these ideas
concerning grace, and thus an incipient "theology of grace"
among the South German Anabaptists was never fully
elaborated.

A most original theology of grace is found in the comprehensive writings of Pilgram Marpeck (d. 1556), also
studied in detail by Alvin Beachy. Grace, according to Marpeck, is the act whereby God renews the divine image in man
and thus makes the believer a participant in the divine nature.
Grace produces a *restoration of man's original nature*, re-
newing his lost faculties and virtues. For man is endowed by
his Creator with "original grace" (*Erbgnade*),[47] an idea
reminiscent of Hubmaier's "uncorrupted spirit," enabling
man to experience regeneration, after which all life becomes
a "walking in grace."[48] Beachy repeats only his sources
by saying that man is born anew *out* of grace, not *from*
grace. Subsequently he is enabled to "participate in the divine
nature."

All this is undoubtedly a correct representation of Anabaptist thought. But one cannot help feeling that the term
"grace" has been used here in a rather broad sense, such as
"creative love" (Menno Simons), "spirit" (Hubmaier), "light"

(Hans Denck, especially in his tract *Von der Ordnung Gottes,*
1527),[49] "divine presence" (the experience of conversion),
and similar terms, but practically never as "favor" or "mercy,"
as was the semantic use within official Protestant theology.
One will therefore readily agree with Walther Köhler that
the concept of grace as held by Hubmaier and his followers
stands in direct opposition to Luther's doctrine of "justification by grace through faith alone"[50] (what Beachy calls
the "forensic" interpretation). The latter view was totally
outside the Anabaptist frame of mind. In fact, they never read
Paul's reference to it through the eyes of an Augustine, and
used the scriptural categories in a totally different context.
Thus, Oosterbaan's claim that theirs was a "theology of grace"
could be somewhat confusing, without a conscious and radical
redefining of the term.

Should we then dismiss this topic? By no means. But we
must keep in mind that in the existential view of Christianity
grace is something different from grace in the theological
Augustinian view. For that reason I suggest using the Greek
term *charisma,* rather than the English or German terms grace
or *Gnade.* Charisma is an endowment: in German it might be
called *Begnadung.* Conrad Grebel, Michael Sattler, Hans
Hut, Jacob Hutter, and many other early leaders were undoubtedly in this sense "charismatic leaders," men endowed
with the inner gift of spiritual vision that enabled them to
function in their new beginning and in their apostolic and
even prophetic leadership. They knew themselves to be
called, and they had no doubt as to the scriptural justification of the new path to be dared in spite of all opposition.
This is an existential situation rather than (with Beachy) ontological. These leaders went through the experience of conversion[51] and *metanoia* (John 3:3). Now it all depends how one
would interpret this extraordinary experience. One might call
it "God dwelt in me," or "the light of God shone in me,"
or "the inner word spoke in me."[52] One could, however, also
say that the grace of God wrought this blessed change. Rebirth
thus might be seen as the result of a special grace of God, the
restoration of our "lost faculties," to quote Hubmaier. For the

rest, all the forensic elements in theology may be passed over
as not pertinent to this vision. Cornelius J.

Dyck wrote correctly in his splendid essay,
"Sinners and Saints" (1962),[53] that every man faces in his own
life both the glory and the potential tragedy of the first
Adam. That idea was not unfamiliar to the dynamic Anabaptists. In an understanding of human life in which original
sin has lost its existential significance (say, as experience of
despair, anxiety, and *Anfechtung*), grace as a "favor" or
"mercy" of the otherwise hidden God (Luther's *Deus Abscondi-
tus)* is no longer relevant. It is simply not experienced that
way.[54]

Grace in the present context is both a uniquely illuminat-
ing experience, and at the same time, its "theological
explanation" or cause. Inasmuch as Anabaptist sources
in the introspective area are almost nonexistent, three non-
Anabaptist testimonials may serve as illustrations of what is
meant by such experiences. The first two come from Quaker
sources of the later seventeenth century and are somewhat
congenial with Anabaptist experiences: "I remember that at
a very early age I experienced *the operation of Divine grace,*
condemning me for evil and inciting me to goodness"; and the
second witness: "being inspired with a *Divine principle* I
felt the power of it overcoming my heart." Later on the same
person writes: "I was sensible of the tending impression of
Divine love."[55]

It is noteworthy that the description of this experience
uses three different terms: grace, divine principle, and divine
love; all three, of course, synonymous. No theology was deduced from such experience.

The third witness is the noted contemporary French
Catholic existentialist Gabriel Marcel, who writes autobio-
graphically almost in the vein of Blaise Pascal: "I have no
more doubts. This morning happiness is miraculous. For
the first time I have clearly experienced *grace.* . . . We
really experience the presence of God."[56] A few pages later
Marcel calls this experience "Truth" and then "Holy Spirit."
Here again we meet the same variety of expressions for the

ineffable. No real "explanation" is tried and no theology founded on these experiences. The Quakers speak generally of the "inner light," and Gabriel Marcel turned religious existentialist. The Anabaptists, not given to this kind of introspection and self-description, are satisfied with confessing, "although we are not perfect we have no doubt concerning God's grace."[57]

In the entire corpus of Anabaptist writings one sole tract deals predominantly with grace, Leonhard Schiemer's profound *Von dreierlei Gnade*, written most likely in the Rattenberg prison in 1527.[58] One has to admit, however, that this remarkable tract, written to the orphaned brotherhood of that Tyrolean mining city as an epistle instructing them on spiritual questions, is as little centered around the theological idea of grace as was the tract "Concerning the Satisfaction of Christ," mentioned in the preceding chapter, dealing with satisfaction. Anabaptist writings were never scholarly structured or otherwise discursive but always of a confessional or testimonial nature. Thus it is not too easy to condense Schiemer's insights on grace into a few propositions. The writer was obviously influenced by Hubmaier's trichotomic anthropology (body, soul, spirit) which he now paraphrased in his own original way, applying it to the idea of grace.

There are three kinds of human beings, Schiemer tells his readers, namely carnal man, lethargic or inert man, and the spiritual or alert man, a most astute distinction indeed. In his epistle he wants to speak only of the third kind of man, assuming that the Anabaptist congregation of Rattenberg was composed mainly of such. And here the "first grace" enters: As soon as such a man experiences "the light of the spirit,"[59] he tries to resist sin but cannot do so out of his own resources. To him God gives grace upon grace to make him strong. The "second grace" is a step further on this spiritual pilgrimage. At one point he calls it righteousness, alluding to the fourth beatitude, "Blessed are those who hunger and thirst after righteousness." And that is precisely the content of the second grace, this ability "to hunger and thirst after righteousness." True grace, however, on this

pilgrimage is recognized in a typically Anabaptist way as
the cross: "For a non-crucified Christian is like untried ore
or like a house where the trees have not yet been cut into
beams."[60] A little earlier he says, "The first light is our taskmaster, but when the spirit of Christ comes into me, then I
am no longer under such a taskmaster but I am now under
grace."[61] Finally, the third grace is called the glorious "anointment" (1 John 2:20, 27) which the believer receives from
God. This "oil" is the Holy Spirit.[62] In other words, the disciple has now overcome all carnal tribulations and is vic-
torious in his final trial. He has become one with Christ.
He will die, but he will also rise with Christ.

That was the spirit of the incipient, still strongly spiritual-
istically oriented, Anabaptist movement. One senses its
tremendous spiritual strength, and will readily forego greater
sharpness of presentation. Grace for these men meant the
inner power to resist sin. It meant also the "inner light"
which enabled the believer to walk the path of righteousness
and to visualize the cross as the likely consequence, interpreting suffering as a step to greater blessedness. At the end one
rightly anticipated the anointment of the Holy Spirit, which
makes man triumphant in all his tribulations and insensitive
to the expected suffering.

Going back to the very beginnings of Anabaptism, we find
Georg (Jörg) Blaurock, one of the three men who started the
movement in Zurich in January 1525. Characteristic of him
is a certain enthusiasm which so completely filled his mind
that he could sing nothing but praise to his Lord who had
blessed him so extraordinarily. The *Martyrs Mirror* of 1660
quotes the following prayer by Blaurock which fittingly concludes this chapter on grace among the Anabaptists.

Lord God, I will praise Thee now and until my end. Thou
hast given me faith. Thou sendest to me Thy divine word
which I am able to find and perceive that it is from pure
grace. From Thee, O God, have I received it as Thou
knowest. My heart rejoices because I know Thy will.

And somewhat later in the same *Martyrs Mirror:*

O Lord, give us true love so to walk that when we come we will not find the door closed. O Zion, thou holy church, see that thou holdest fast unto the end, and keep thyself unspotted from sins, and thou shalt, through grace, receive the eternal crown.[63]

Grace here is the equivalent of an inner, spiritual illumination (which five or eight years later the Swiss Brethren no longer accepted, in fact even opposed), an ineffable "knowledge" of God's will. And this understanding of charismatic experience as inner *knowledge* we meet once more with the next great witness of early Anabaptism, Michael Sattler, certainly a crown witness to the genius of Anabaptism.[64] In his exhortative epistle to his brethren in Horb in Württemberg, written in prison in 1527, and later widely distributed as a pamphlet, we find the following impressive passage: "Be shining lights whom God has illuminated with His knowledge and the light of His Spirit."[65]

In reading these testimonials one cannot help but recall the documents of the primitive or apostolic church, the similarity of the two periods being truly striking. The existential genuineness of these testimonials cannot be doubted.

Footnotes to "Soteriology"

1. In contrast, Pietists and holiness groups tried to force such a "conversion" by means of a previous *Busskampf* or struggle for repentance, hence the term "Methodism" in English church history. Such a methodic producing of quasi-spiritual experiences, however, was totally foreign to Anabaptists. A very lively picture of the spontaneity of such experiences at the beginning of the movement is presented by Fritz Blanke in his small but delightful book *Brothers in Christ* (Scottdale, 1960; Eng. ed. of *Brüder in Christo; die Geschichte der ältesten Täufergemeinde, Zollikon, 1525,* Zürich, 1955).

2. Peter Rideman, *Account of Our Religion* (1950), 36.

3. Peter Walpot, *The Great Article Book of 1577,* The Third Article of which was published in an English translation under the title, "A Notable Hutterite Document: Concerning True Surrender and Christian Community of Goods," *MQR,* XXXI (1957). Our quotation is from "Point 38," p. 33.

4. See above, pp. 71 f., 73. Cf. also my essay, "The Christian Communism of the Hutterite Brethren," *ARG,* XLVI (1955), particularly p. 207.

5. George H. Williams, ed., *Spiritual and Anabaptist Writers* (Library of Christian Classics, XXV) (1957), 80, and *passim.* See also Harold S. Bender, *Conrad Grebel* (1950), 179, 206.

6. Harold S. Bender at the Sixth Mennonite World Conference. See *MQR,* XXXVI (1962), 201.

7. Wiswedel, *Bilder und Führergestalten aus dem Täufertum,* II (1930), 197.

8. *Ibid.* Concerning the idea of "Descensus ad Inferos" see "Nicodemus" by William Klassen, *ME*, III, 871, 872, and George H. Williams, *The Radical Reformation* (1962), 840-842.

9. "Man muss durch diese Tiefe hindurchgehen, wenn man durch Christus erlöst werden will." Müller, *Glaubenszeugnisse*, 36.

10. *Kunstbuch*, 1561, No. 35 (ms. copy at Goshen College Mennonite Historical Library). See Heinold Fast in *ARG* (1956), 216, 235. Here *Tiefe* means lowliness, voluntary self-humiliation, *kenosis* (Phil. 2:7).

11. Williams, *Radical Reformation*, 861.

12. "Concerning the Satisfaction of Christ," introduced and translated by J. C. Wenger, *MQR*, XX (1946), 247-254.

13. *Ibid.*, 250-252.

14. *Täuferakten, Baden-Pfalz*, ed. Manfred Krebs (1951), 113, 114. The second part of Thesis Seven reads similarly: "Thus the physical suffering of Jesus is not the true satisfaction toward the Father and reconciliation with the Father without our own inner obedience and our highest desire to obey the eternal will of God Almighty" (*Ibid.*, 114). Martin Bucer's answer called *Getrewe Warnung* may be found in *Täuferakten, Elsass* I, 1959, No. 86, 105 ff., where the articles are presented first by Kautz and then the rejoinder by Bucer.

15. Paul Wappler, *Stellung Kursachsens* (1910), 197.

16. Müller, *Glaubenszeugnisse*, 66. In German: "Es ist Got seiner allmechtigkeit nach nit müglich, das er mich on creütz seelig mach...."

17. Ambrosius Spittelmaier, 1527. See *Täuferakten, Bayern I* (ed. Schornbaum), 51. In a free English translation: "Christ, true God and man, the head of all his members, has erased with his suffering the eternal wrath of God against us. He has reconciled us and restored us to peace with God. His suffering and death have opened for us the kingdom from which we had fallen because of Adam." He then argues that man must not only believe this but also be willing to go the same way. See *MQR*, XXXIII (1959), 288 f.

18. Johann Loserth, *Pilgram Marpecks Antwort auf Kaspar Schwenckfelds Beurteilung des Buches der Bundesbezeugung von 1542* (1929), Introduction, p. 34.

19 *Thomas Müntzer, sein Leben und seine Schriften*, ed. O. Brandt (1933), 129.

20. See Friedmann, "Concerning a True Soldier of Christ, *MQR*, V (1931), 87-99. For more references see my article, "Sweet or Bitter Christ," *ME*, IV, 668-669.

21. "Denn er anderst denn durch Kreuz und Leiden nit kann selig werden." L. Müller, *Glaubenszeugnisse*, 95. One is reminded here of the saying in John 12:24, "Except a corn of wheat fall into the ground and die, it abideth alone. But if it die it bringeth forth much fruit."

22. So, for instance, George H. Williams, W. Wiswedel, Hans J. Hillerbrand, Hans G. Fischer, Harold S. Bender, Alvin Beachy, and Herbert Klassen.

23. Martin Luther, *Briefwechsel*, Weimar Edition, No. 428, 383.

24. Dietrich Bonhoeffer, *Cost of Discipleship* (1949), 45, 46.

25. Harold S. Bender insists also on this distinction as a precondition to a correct understanding of the doctrine of justification. See, e.g., his excellent article, "Perfectionism," *ME*, IV, 1115.

26. Which term, when translated as "making pious," would not render the proper meaning. *Fromm-Machen* means rather "making God-fearing," or still better, "making just or aright."

27. Hans J. Hillerbrand, "Anabaptism and Reformation: Another Look," *Church History* (1960), 413, where he interprets justification in Anabaptist texts as a "covenant wherein God offers His grace through Jesus Christ, and man pledges to desist from sin and follow God." Strictly speaking, this covenant is not "justification" in the conventional sense of the term. Its place would rather be in baptismal theology according to 1 Peter 3:21.

100   The Theology of Anabaptism

28. Hillerbrand, *loc. cit.*, claims that the Council of Trent (1545-63) likewise accepted this idea of *Fromm-Machung* in response to the challenge of the Protestant theology of justification.

29. Balthasar Hubmaier, *Schriften*, ed. Bergsten (1962), 157-163, 109 f.

30. *Ibid.*, 316.

31. *Wasser aller Trübsalen*, obviously alluding to Acts 14:22, "We must through much tribulation enter into the kingdom of God." "Water" refers, of course, to the pledge at baptism.

32. Müller, *Glaubenszeugnisse*, 20, 21.

33. *Ibid.*, 23.

34. Herbert Klassen, "The Life and Teachings of Hans Hut," *MQR*, XXXIII (1959), 288, 292.

35. Peter Rideman, *Account* (1950), 35.

36. What Dietrich Bonhoeffer would most likely call "cheap grace."

37. *Das Kunstbuch*, No. 32, fol. 255b. Typescript copy at Goshen College Mennonite Historical Library.

38. Harold S. Bender, "Pilgram Marpeck," etc. *MQR*, XXXVIII (1964), 262.

39. *MQR*, XXVIII (1954), 27-38.

40. *Ibid.*, 37.

41. *Ibid.*, 33.

42. The first to do so was J. C. Wenger of Goshen Biblical Seminary in a study on "Grace and Discipleship in Anabaptism," *MQR*, XXXV (1961), 50-69. The paper deals, however, nearly exclusively with the theology of Menno Simons, and thus lies outside the scope of the present study. The next was Alvin J. Beachy, whose dissertation (1960) dealt with precisely this idea of grace within South German Anabaptism. Beachy's professor thought he would come to a negative conclusion, namely, that grace is not an essential term in Anabaptist thinking. Happily, it turned out otherwise. Beachy condensed his work for the *MQR* (1963), dealing with the theology of Menno Simons and Dirck Philips, as well as that of Melchior Hofmann, Hans Denck, Pilgram Marpeck, and Balthasar Hubmaier. We shall in part follow Beachy's lead. The *Festschrift* for Cornelius Krahn, *A Legacy of Faith* (1962), also contains a most stimulating essay by J. A. Oosterbaan, Mennonite professor at the University of Amsterdam, entitled "Grace in Dutch Mennonite Theology." The author concludes somewhat like Wenger that Menno Simons' theology was basically a theology of grace. See pp. 69-85. Oosterbaan warns us, however, that nearly all theological terms change in their traditional meanings when used by "theologically inexperienced Anabaptists."

43. Exceptions: Luke 2:4 and John 1:11, 16, 17.

44. Oosterbaan, *op. cit.*, 77, 78.

45. *Ibid.*, 79, 82, 84-85.

46. I wonder whether "ontological" is not meant here in the same sense as I am using the term "existential." Beachy speaks also of "divinization" (*Vergöttlichung*) in the sense of the Johannine Gospel which, however, is hardly a genuine Anabaptist term.

47. Pilgram Marpeck's *Verantwortung*, ed. Loserth (above, Note 18), 204, 206. Marpeck uses three different terms: *Erbgnade* (p. 206), *Gegenerb* (p. 204), and *Gestrige Gnade* (p. 202).

48. Michael Sattler called it "Wandlen in der uffersteeung" (walking in the resurrection); Beatrice Jenny, *Das Schleitheimer Täuferbekenntnis, 1527* (Schaffhausen, 1951), 10, 1. 63.

49. Hans Denck, *Ordnung Gottes und der Creaturen Werk*, 1527, ed. Walter Fellmann (1956), 87-103. On page 96 we read, most characteristically, "Welcher sagt, er hab nit Gnad von Gott, fromb zu werden, der ist eyn lugner." This is, in brief, the gist of Anabaptist teaching on grace.

50. Walther Köhler, *Dogmengeschichte als Geschichte des christlichen Selbstbe-*

wusstseins, II: *Das Zeitalter der Reformation* (1951), 358.

51. See Myron S. Augsburger, "Conversion in Anabaptist Theology," *MQR*, XXXVI (1962), 243 ff.

52. Rufus M. Jones, *Spiritual Reformers of the Sixteenth Century* (1914, 2nd. ed., 1928). Jones saw the early Anabaptists as forerunners of the Quakers of the later seventeenth century. This is a correct judgment if we think of Hans Denck, but it would hardly fit the Anabaptists after say 1531/2. See also Wiswedel's fine study, "The Inner and the Outer Word, etc.," *MQR*, XXVI (1952), 171 ff., and "Inneres Licht," *Mennonitisches Lexikon* (hereafter *ML*), II, 420, 421.

53. C. J. Dyck, "Sinners and Saints," in *A Legacy of Faith* (1962), 94.

54. Hence the omission in both *ME* and *ML*.

55. Howard Brinton, *Friends for 300 Years* (1952), one of the best books on Quakerism.

56. Gabriel Marcel, *Being and Having*, 15, 22.

57. Hutterite Epistle to Simon Ronemberg of Cracow, 1570, in A. J. F. Zieglschmid, ed., *Die älteste Chronik* (1943), 453.

58. Müller, *Glaubenszeugnisse*, 58-71, minus 68-69. See above, Part I, footnote 12.

59. This is a Johannine term used only in early Anabaptist tracts.

60. Müller, *Glaubenszeugnisse*, 67. The parable of the house, the tree, and the beam originated with Hans Hut, *ibid.*, 33. The same parable is also used by Peter Riedemann in his so-called "Gmundener Rechenschaft" of 1530/3, in *Glaubenszeugnisse oberdeutscher Taufgesinnter*, II (ed., L. Müller and Robert Friedmann), 1967, 23.

61. *Ibid.*, 66.

62. *Ibid.*, 70.

63. See Orley Swartzentruber, "The Piety and Theology of the Anabaptist Martyrs in van Braght's *Martyrs Mirror*," *MQR*, XXVIII (1954), 24, 25. The entire study is first-rate and deserves a careful reading. I followed Swartzentruber's quotations.

64. [See the splendid fresh translation and interpretation of Sattler by John H. Yoder: *The Legacy of Michael Sattler* (Scottdale, Pa.: Herald Press, 1973). JCW.]

65. *Ibid.*, 18, 19. It is also worthwhile to look up the moving epistles of Anneken Jans of Rotterdam, 1539, also taken from the *Martyrs Mirror*, in which the spirit of discipleship and obedience find a superb expression.

D

Eschatology:
Preparedness for the Kingdom of God

It is a well-known fact that the early period of the Age of the Reformation (c. 1520-35) was strongly eschatologically oriented. To a Martin Luther the Book of Daniel was a real "comforter in these last days," and his co-workers Melanchthon, Osiander, and Oecolampad felt similarly. To wide circles the pope was the anti-Christ predicted in the Book of Revelation, and was so pictured in the pamphlet literature of the time. Everyone felt deeply the current "crisis" in history and read the Apocalypse with intense anticipation. It was a time of tremendous spiritual alertness. Luther, who believed in the hiddenness of the true church of God, was fully aware of the power of Satan here on earth; hence his longing for the "*liebe jüngste Tag.*" He lived for a while in an intense eschatological consciousness of the historical process currently taking place. In fact, he impatiently proclaimed that "we are in God's kingdom,"[1] though he knew very well the great obstacles still to be overcome. But could not the *parousia* (second coming) of the Savior be imminent? The end of history, judgment day, the fulfillment of time, the parousia and the kingdom of God — the latter imagined either as "eternal life" or, as the "new world" (2 Peter 3:13): this sequence was alertly anticipated as God's plan or "economy" now.

Nevertheless, this eschatological mood did not generally lead the Reformers to concrete speculations as to the date of such a cataclysmic change. Such speculations, combined usually with violent enthusiasm to accelerate the coming of the event, did actually occur in the days of the Peasants' War and Thomas Müntzer, and after that time all those who opposed the Lutheran innovations were anathematized as *Schwärmer.* Both the *Confessio Augustana* (§ 17) and the *Confessio Helvetica* (§ 11) condemn this kind of chiliasm or "Jewish dreaming."[2] Not long thereafter the eschatological mood faded away in the official state churches, and the ensuing "orthodox" Protestant theology tended to ignore the idea of a "second coming" of Christ, concentrating basically on the theme of personal certitude of salvation (*Heilsgewissheit*). There was simply no room left for a meaningful eschatology within the late Lutheran and post-Lutheran theology. The only place where such ideas were kept alive and had a legitimate function was the "left wing" of the Reformation or, as we now call it, the Radical Reformation: Anabaptism and related movements.

Here the "theology of the kingdom," as we have developed it earlier in this study, logically also implied the expectation of the *imminence* of the coming of the kingdom. This in turn released new energies, mainly in the form of a tremendous missionary zeal, practically unknown within the official territorial Protestant churches. It was the Lutheran theologian Paul Althaus who in his outstanding book *Die letzten Dinge*[3] unreservedly gave credit to the Anabaptists for this new element. He makes a surprising assertion:

> In their zeal for mission the chiliasm of the Anabaptists had as its inner truth the expression of the fact that the coming of the New Earth and the proclaiming of the good news to all men are closely connected. Chiliasm has its clear justification in accepting responsibility in the here and now for concentrating all activities on the coming kingdom.[4]

And a few lines later he is still more outspoken, even though he is in general not at all interested in left-wing studies:

> Chiliasm has to be understood concretely[5] as guardian of the authentic realism of the expectation and responsibility vis-à-vis the mystical-spiritualistic abandonment of this world here. For chiliasm means also *to remain faithful to this earth;* that is, it means working toward the overcoming of the demons of this world.

Coming from a respected Protestant theologian these are quite remarkable words,[6] and they encourage us to investigate further the ideas of those "Radical Reformers" to whom Althaus gave so much credit.

Turning to a more systematic treatment of eschatological ideas in Anabaptism (which are part of their implicit theology), we must sharply distinguish between two aspects of the subject:

(1) The concrete or existential eschatological expectation, the actual living in anticipation of the *parousia*. This may happen in two ways: (a) as "quiet eschatology," or an inner preparation of oneself for the expected coming of the kingdom. In this connection we shall emphasize in particular the misssionary activities of the brethren. And (b) as "violent eschatology," conventionally also called "chiliasm" proper, which in history is represented mainly by the figure of Thomas Müntzer or the events in the city of Münster, for which

phenomena the German word *Schwärmer* seems to be quite appropriate. A characteristic of chiliasm is a reliance on prophecies and calculations, a very common phenomenon in history.[7] This type we will not enlarge upon.

(2) The other aspect of eschatological thinking is of a quite different nature, a sort of literary use of the Book of Revelation and the imagery of the Apocalypse. The Scriptures have such apocalypses in the Synoptics, Matthew 24, Mark 13, and Luke 21; in the Book of Daniel, the basic book of this type; and in the Book of Revelation; besides the numerous apocryphal apocalypses such as the Fourth Book of Esdras, popular with the Anabaptists, who found it in the Vulgate and the Froschauer Bible but not in the Luther version. The imagery of these books was much liked and used for an interpretation of history and its "true" periodization. Of course, such ideas were very common in the first decades of the Reformation and may be encountered in Lutheran writings, as well as in Anabaptist tracts,[8] for this kind of historical thinking was then very popular and appealing.

A survey of the entire history of Anabaptism of the sixteenth century yields, to our amazement, very little in way of a radical, eschatological nature. Of course, Münster is the one glaring exception, condemned by the overwhelming majority of Anabaptists, the quiet or evangelical Anabaptists, as they are usually called. They repudiated any rebellious action or use of violence for the promotion of the kingdom on earth. Strictly speaking we know of only two men among the first-generation Anabaptists who leaned toward an outspoken and passionate eschatology: Hans Hut (and a few followers) and Melchior Hofmann (and some followers).[9] Inasmuch as Hofmann's activities pertained mainly to North German and Dutch areas which lie beyond the field of our study, the entire discussion is reduced to the activities of Hans Hut only.

Hut was a passionate apostle of Anabaptism. Profound and effective, he was a real leader who in the brief span of his Anabaptist activities (1526-27) achieved the remarkable rise of the movement in Bavaria, Franconia, Austria (mainly Upper Austria), and even Moravia. His figure looms high in the ongoing movement and his ideas were germinal for decades to come. Without Hut Anabaptism would not have been what it was, at least in the South German area. The caliber of his followers (among whom we meet Ambrosius Spittelmaier, Leonhard Schiemer, Hans Schlaffer, Hans Nadler; also Wolfgang Brandhuber and Oswald Glaidt, and to a certain degree even Pilgram Marpeck)[10] speaks well for Hut as an "apostle"[11] of the Anabaptists. He was a creative inspiring personality who enriched Anabaptism in many ways.

To characterize Hut within the present context is by no means simple, in part because the sources are incomplete. To call Hut a Müntzerite would be unfair even though some Müntzerite viewpoints remained with Hut after his profound "conversion" in 1526 under the influence of Hans Denck. From then on he repudiated all Müntzerite *Schwärmer*-tendencies; above all, any efforts toward a violent overthrow of the "godless" princes, and the ushering in of the kingdom by way of the sword. Much has been written about Hut,[12] and the interpretation of his work oscillates according to the view of the authors. Only two tracts by Hut are known,[13] and both are profound and spiritual. But they say nothing regarding "the last things." His frequently quoted epistle of 1527,[14] a sort of circular letter to the brethren everywhere in South Germany, expresses his willingness to desist from propagating openly his eschatological visions unless asked about them. This remarkable promise he seems to have made at the renowned "Martyrs' Synod" at Augsburg in August 1527, apparently at the request of the majority present, just one month prior to his arrest in the same city. That the brethren prevailed upon him in this regard, most likely under the leadership of Hans Denck, whose thinking was certainly a far cry from all apocalypticism, is a strong indication that the majority of Anabaptists did not favor any "chiliastic" attitude or calculations. They preferred the "quiet eschatology" of both withdrawal (thus creating small nuclei of saints ready for the kingdom whenever it might come) and an intense mission work to increase the number of genuine disciples for the kingdom.

In this regard — that is, in the opposition to prophecy and historical calculations .and with them some form of promotional activities — an observation by Lydia Müller sheds some light on the mind of these brethren. Müller published Leonhard Schiemer's *Eine hüpsche Erklerung der XII Articl des christlichen Glaubens* (c. 1527), which contains a meditation on Daniel's prophecy of the coming of the kingdom in three and a half years.[15] That this was a point of Hut's teaching is known from several sources, for instance from Hubmaier's *Rechenschaft* of January 1528.[16] But then a footnote to this passage mentions that another Hutterite codex with the same Schiemer tract omits this particular section,[17] obviously because the Hutterite copyist (of a later decade) was not in sympathy with this kind of thinking. And as late as 1962, the same thing happened with the only millenarian hymn in the *Lieder der Hutterischen Brüder*, entitled "Vom Neuen Jerusalem."[18] When a new edition or reprint of this hymnal was planned recently, this hymn was the only omission in the entire book. "We do not believe in the idea of the millennium," the Hutterites wrote me, "hence we did not want to reprint this hymn in our new hymnal."

What do we actually know about Hans Hut's "chiliasm" since the sources are so reticent? Mainly through confessions of his followers do we gain a glimpse of certain aspects of his teachings. Since these confessions are in harmony with one another, we may justly assume that these were Hut's own ideas. There was above all the item called *Sieben Urteile*,[19] supposedly going back to the Hut-Hubmaier debate at Nicolsburg in May 1527. These *Sieben Urteile* deal with (1) the divine covenant, (2) kingdom of God, (3) body of Christ [the church], (4) end of the world, (5) coming judgment, (6) resurrection of the body, and (7) the eternal verdict. Besides these points the Turkish threat was interpreted as a sign of God's imminent judgment, recalling similar warnings by the prophet Jeremiah. These *Sieben Urteile* seem to have been widely broadcast. Two of Hut's followers mentioned them at their trials: Ambrosius Spittelmaier in 1527,[20] and Hans Nadler in 1529.[21] On the other hand, Hans Schlaffer, although a Hut convert, was in his thinking closer to Denck than to Hut and definitely objected to this kind of eschatological speculation. The main question, however, is still to be clarified: is it really correct to claim (as some authors do) that Hut was merely a "Thomas Müntzer in disguise"? Was he so filled with this anticipation of the coming catastrophe, of the near parousia of Christ on earth and of the establishment of His kingdom, that he made this the very core of his message? Or was he actually nearer to the basic Anabaptist vision of discipleship which had little connection with this kind of speculation? The answer is to be found in a remark by Hut at his trial at Augsburg on November 4, 1527, where he testified that he had *"assembled his views out of the Scriptures for the consolation of those who are persecuted so that they may perceive the reward that is bound to come to them in the next world."*[22] This sounds in no way reminiscent of Thomas Müntzer. In fact, it appears as a concern of a genuinely apostolic nature and should make us appreciate Hut's version of Anabaptist eschatology all the more. But it is also true that this "version" of Hut disappeared soon after his death, giving room to a different bent of mind: a "quiet eschatology," to which we now turn.

An observation by a foremost expert of Anabaptist hymnody may serve as introduction. Rosella Reimer Duerksen writes about the doctrinal implications in Anabaptist hymns as follows:

> Throughout Reformation hymnody runs the overtone of the belief in an imminent eschatology. That the dangerous emphasis on chiliasm did not capture the heart of the Anabaptist movement is attested by the fact that vicious militant plans for the ushering in of the Kingdom of God are *nowhere* reflected in the printed Anabaptist hymn collections. Even the hymn ascribed to Hans Hut (found in the *Ausbund* and *Lieder der Hutterischen Brüder*) gives no indication of his chiliastic tendencies. It is also significant to note that not a single one of the hymns of Thomas Müntzer was adopted for use in Anabaptist collections.[23]

From the many passages expressing this mood of "quiet

eschatology" we will present two examples, one from the very
early time, 1527; and another, eleven years later, 1538, to illustrate the spiritual climate of those times. When Michaél
Sattler, certainly one of the strongest and noblest leaders
of the Swiss Brethren in South Germany, was arrested in
1527, he dispatched a letter to the brotherhood of Horb in
Württemberg, one of the finest in the long line of Anabaptist
epistles. Combined in a pamphlet with his witness at his
trial and the story of his final execution, it was widely distributed all over the country, including Moravia, and was
also incorporated into the Dutch *Martyrs Mirror* (1660).
One characteristic passage of this memorable document
follows:

> Beloved brethren, pray that the reapers will be compelled
> to go to the harvest, for the time of threshing is imminent.
> The abomination of destruction has come clearly into the
> open and the elected servants and handmaidens of God
> will be signed on their foreheads with the name of their
> Father. The world in its erring is getting aroused against
> the redeemed, but these give testimony to the gospel be-
> fore all the world as witnesses. And thereafter it will be
> high time that the Day of the Lord will not tarry.[24]

One clearly senses here the feeling of urgency, a cry to
God: *Es wird Not sein, dass sich des Herren Tag nicht verlängere.* For how could the children of the Lord endure all
that horrible persecution for a prolonged period? This mood,
however, leads only to a call to give testimony and to remain
steadfast in all that abomination of a world which is possessed
by the "Prince of Darkness." And then Sattler quotes as his
reference — not Matthew 24, and Revelation 13 or 16, but —
the apocryphal Fourth Book of Esdras in the translation of
Leo Jud found in the Zürich Froschauer Bible, which as a
genuine apocalypse announces "the nearness of the kingdom
of God, comforting the faithful to stand all that hardship for
but a little while. The Saviour will not tarry too long."
    Eleven years later and in less oppressive Moravia, the
Hutterite elders under the leadership of Hans Amon com-

posed a missive to a brother in Hesse, Mathes Hasenhan, which also reflects the mood of "quiet eschatology," the expectation of the end of the world and the nearness of the second coming of the Lord. This time the passion of urgency had faded away and the tone had mellowed, even though the awareness of living in a period of crisis lingered on. The Hutterites wrote to Hesse in 1538:

> We wait and prepare ourselves in patience, truth, and godliness for the instant when the King and Bridegroom is to appear from heaven together with the angels of His power, to give vengeance with flaming fire to all those who have not become obedient to His word. And then we will be found saintly and blameless before Him and may have all confidence that we will enter together with Him into the glory and joy of eternity.[25]

The tone has changed somewhat but the spirit is the same: have confidence in God's final justice, be comforted in this hope and in the glorious expectation of a new day.

Time and again we read similar passages in Anabaptist epistles. The characteristic form, "in these last and most dangerous times (or days)," occurs frequently, reflecting a consciousness that this was a time of crisis in God's plan. "Be on the alert" was the watchword among the brethren. "Do not be lethargic," Jacob Hutter warned his "dear children," and he continued, "do not act like the foolish maidens in the parable who had no oil in their lamps when the bridegroom arrived at midnight." In this sense eschatology assumes a quasi-existential quality among the brethren, not only in Moravia but throughout South and Central Germany.[26]

For a long time I did not fully grasp this eschatological aspect in Anabaptist theology. Since the sources hardly ever elaborate on apocalyptic ideas, and since chiliasm was repudiated as early as the Martyrs' Synod of August 1527, I tended to consider eschatological categories as merely marginal in Anabaptist theology, as a call to alertness and preparedness for the Lord's second coming. But I did not feel the excitement, the impatient waiting for deliverance as com-

pared with other periods of history when people were count-
ing the days until the great change.[27] But a deeper search
into the "implicit" theology of Anabaptism taught me otherwise. On the basis of all the evidence this new understanding
may be formulated somewhat as follows:

(a) Eschatology is part and parcel of the "theology of the
kingdom" which represents the very center of Anabaptist
thinking and believing. The kingdom (and *not merely personal salvation*) is the real concern of the reborn disciples
of Christ. This kingdom may have become realized already in
the small brotherhoods which sprang up everywhere, nuclei
of brotherly love and sharing, where hatred and violence
were absent as far as humanly attainable, and where sin
was fought as well as possible. Or, this kingdom is still
coming, though its contours have already become perceptible,
and the brethren were trying to prepare themselves for it by
all that was described above. It gave spiritual strength and
that kinds of alertness which speaks so clearly in all documents,
above all in those of the first generation up to about 1550/60.

(b) Eschatology is also the background of the extraordinary
Anabaptist *zeal for mission*, which was so little known within
sixteenth-century Protestantism. Only those, they claim,
who have in obedience surrendered to the will of God will see
the kingdom, while all the others will be crushed by God's
judgment on the last day. There is no threatening tone in this
Anabaptist outreach. But the fact remains that the missioners, called *Sendboten*, were dispatched to all corners of
Europe, from Switzerland to Denmark, from the Rhine to
Poland and Hungary, and worked undauntedly against tremendous odds. This fact alone deserves attention and proper
interpretation.[28] Of course, all mission work derives from
that Great Commission of Christ which applies to all times
Still, it appears that in the beginning of the Anabaptist movement the conviction was strongest that "only those who belong
to the true church could expect grace on the Day of Judgment."
That the bulk of all mission activities was carried out by the
Hutterites is true but can be easily explained by the fact, that
only the Hutterites had well-organized and fairly stable broth-

erhood-churches (*Gemeinden*) in Moravia, while the Swiss Brethren, and for a while also the Marpeck brotherhood, struggled for survival and could hardly afford efficient outreach, except for the very early years when enthusiasm was stronger than all handicaps.

As stated earlier in this chapter, there are two possible approaches to the topic of eschatology. One of them understands eschatology as a vital force influencing man's action, separating him from the world and sending him out to proselytize, to call people to repentance and discipleship. The other is of a more literary nature. People of all times have been fond of using the imagery of the apocalypse and developed a new vision of the course of man's history (*Heilsgeschichte*). For the gist of all apocalypses is a sort of "philosophy of history," ever since the Book of Daniel, or perhaps even earlier if we think of the vision of Hebrew prophets of the "peaceful kingdom of the Messiah" at the end of history.

At a rather early time, around 1530, the Hutterites got hold of a little-known book of medieval origin which contained an exposition or commentary of the Book of Revelation, namely, Petrus Olivi's *Postil on the Apocalypse*, written in 1295/96 by the leader of the Spiritual Franciscans who had come under the influence of Joachim de Floris (d. 1202), the renowned prophet of the coming of the "Age of the Spirit." The fact that this interesting book has survived more than four hundred years of Anabaptist history and is still being copied and read by the Hutterite brethren in America, speaks strongly for its appeal.[29] True, the Hutterites never deliver a sermon on the last book of the Bible, for they do not foster an apocalyptic spirit, but they copied the *Postil* again and again in a number of handwritten devotional codices and even gave its author a niche in their great chronicle, the *Geschichtsbuch*. It is conjectured that the "philosophy" of this book found a strong echo among the

Anabaptists mainly for one reason: it deals with the struggle between the "church of the clerics" and the "church of the Spirit" in this, the third and final period of sacred history. Only by persecution and martyrdom, and obeying apostolic poverty, can genuine evangelical life prosper. In this Joachimite picture the church of Rome assumes more and more the character of the anti-Christ. Rome is "Babylon," the "Synagogue of the Devil." Thus the Spiritual Franciscans denied to Rome any justification for existence in the on-going drama of sacred history, and predicted its fall and replacement by the "Church of the Spirit."[30] It appears that this stigmatization of Rome reverberated also in Anabaptist thinking and gave meaning to Anabaptist activities and suffering. This kind of speculation was not a causal factor in the great upheaval of the 1520s, but it somehow supported it and made it more meaningful with the masses.

Thus, for instance, the remarkable tract by the Tyrolean Anabaptist Ulrich Stadler, *Von der Gemeinschaft der Heiligen,* c. 1536, contains passages in which the pope is again called "the Babylonian whore who sits on the dragon with the seven heads, the synagogue of the living devil, etc.,"[31] strongly reminiscent of Olivi's *Postil.* This apocalyptic imagery, which was popular in those days, does not in itself prove any active eschatology among the brethren but it lends some support to our earlier observations.

Also around 1530 an anonymous pamphlet of Anabaptist origin was published, probably in Augsburg, which shows the same kind of imagery. It is the treatise on the Christian and the state, entitled *Aufdeckung der Babylonischen Hurn und Antichrists alter und newer geheimnus und grewel,* etc.,[32] its frontispiece showing the "harlot" on the beast with seven heads (Revelation 13 — 17), then a rather popular mockery of the church of Rome. Again it does not prove much but simply illustrates the general frame of mind of that time where the vocabulary of the Book of Revelation was used not only in a merely polemical vein but with an inner acceptance of the implied philosophy of history. Exactly the same observation may be made by studying a tract mentioned earlier, *Von der Genugthuung Christi* (1527/30) — it too exhibits the same vocabulary or imagery. After criticizing all of contemporary Christendom, it continues: "And how well one can see here the beast that has seven heads and ten horns (Revelation 13:1), which has recovered from its deadly wounds inasmuch as the Romish school is again defended as the truth by the scribes." And then it mentions "the second beast with two horns, and the ten horns on the beast which hate the whore. . . . And the kingdom would be given to the beast until the Word of God should be fulfilled (Revelation 17:17)."[33]

All these examples derive from the earliest period. After about 1540, we hardly meet anything of this character. The eschatological mood had vanished and was replaced by a more evangelical frame of mind oriented toward *Nachfolge*. The "enthusiastic" interpretation of history gave way to a quiet eschatology which was no longer time-bound, though not less vital in theology and missionary zeal.

Walther Köhler, in his profound study (1925) of the early Zurich Anabaptists, had already observed that the founders of Anabaptism such as Grebel, Mantz, and Blaurock were filled with a "primitive-chiliastic eschatology."[34] "The kingdom of God is here," said Grebel, filled with a primitive Christian ecstasy as if the Messiah were already present. Others of his company were excited by their anticipation of the last judgment which was to break in at any moment. In fact, the records of these early Anabaptists[35] overflow with such visions of the "end of history" and the coming judgment day. That day can be escaped only by accepting baptism upon faith. "Whosoever refuses this step," said Blaurock, "is a pagan and a child of perdition." That was the beginning in Zurich. As we have seen, it was the same everywhere though not always as enthusiastic as it was with Georg Blaurock. But even when this excitement calmed down, was there not reason enough to read one's gospel from the aspect of Matthew 24 or Luke 21? If a man went through the shaking experience of inner or spiritual rebirth he became conscious of the fact that this "world" would never lead to the hoped-for kingdom of God. Then a radical dualism would develop in which kingdom and "world" represent opposite poles. They committed themselves to the kingdom, and the eschatological framework became operative. "Be ready and be on the alert, fight sin and prepare yourself for the kingdom which is both coming and, as a possibility, is already here." This was a glorious outlook and goes a long way to explain why Anabaptists so courageously defied torture and death. They felt the great promise on their side. And they began to build up a new, "true" church of the Spirit, the subject of the next and final chapter.

Footnotes to "Eschatology"

1. Luther, Werke, Weimar Edition, II, 98.
2. This was previous to the events of Münster, 1534-35.
3. Paul Althaus, Die letzten Dinge (1928).
4. Paul Althaus, "Eschatologie," Religion in Geschichte und Gegenwart (1928), v. II, column 361.
5. Could we not use at this place the better term "existential"?
6. Althaus used some even stronger words in favor of the left-wing groups in the last chapter of Die letzten Dinge (see note 3). It is remarkable indeed that this book went through not less than eight editions.
7. See the widely acclaimed study by Norman Cohn, The Pursuit of the Millennium, now in Harper's Torchbook series, No. 1037.
8. For instance in the title of the early pamphlet Aufdeckung der Babylonischen Hurn, etc., see Hillerbrand, "An Early Anabaptist Treatise, etc.," MQR, XXXII (1958), 28-47. See also below, note 32.
9. Also Bernt Rothmann of Münster might be mentioned, but he certainly does not belong to the company of evangelical Anabaptists.
10. One tract by Hans Hut is also found in the Kunstbuch of 1561 of the Marpeck brotherhood, but the text was slightly amended.
11. I do not use the term "missionary," as he was closer to the New Testament type of an "apostle."
12. See works by Neuser, Klassen, Armour, Stayer, etc.
13. Coming from Hutterite sources and the above-mentioned version in the Kunstbuch (note 10).
14. Hans Hut's epistle is published in Lydia Müller, Glaubenszeugnisse, p. 12.
15. Ibid., 55 f. Hut had predicted that the great cataclysmic event would occur in 1528!
16. Balthasar Hubmaier, Schriften, ed. T. Bergsten (1962), 475.
17. Müller, Glaubenszeugnisse, 56.
18. Die Lieder der Hutterischen Brüder (1914), 419-422.
19. Täuferakten Bayern I, ed. Schornbaum, 49, 50. English translation in MQR, XXXII (1958), 270, 271.
20. Herbert Klassen, "Ambrosius Spittelmaier: Life and Teachings," MQR, XXXII (1958), 263, 265, and note 92. See also Klassen's "Study on Hans Hut." MQR, XXXIII (1959), 201.
21. Täuferakten Bayern I, 153. The "Sieben Urteile" as reported by Hans Nad-

ler do not completely agree with the "Sieben Urteile" as given by Ambrosius Spittelmaier (above, note 19).

22. Christian Meyer, "Die Wiedertäufer in Augsburg," *Zeitschrift des Historischen Vereins für Schwaben und Neuburg*, I (1874), 234. The reference here pertains to the so-called *Ratsbüchlein*, a Bible concordance; in 1527, a completely new type of literature.

23. Rosella Reimer Duerksen, "Doctrinal Implications in Sixteenth Century Anabaptist Hymnody," *MQR*, XXXV (1961), 38. The only millenarian hymn, "Das Neue Jerusalem," *Lieder der Hutterischen Brüder* (1914), 419-422, might have crept into one of the Hutterite hymnal codices from some outside source. The origin is not known.

24. "Brüderliche Vereinigung etzlicher Kinder Gottes, sieben Artikel betreffend," ed., Walter Köhler, in *Flugschriften aus den ersten Jahren der Reformation* (1908), 46. Wenger's English translation has been reprinted many times. The latest translation is by John H. Yoder, published in *The Legacy of Michael Sattler*, Scottdale, Pa.: Herald Press, 1973.

25. Günther Franz, *Urkundliche Quellen zur Hessischen Reformationsgeschichte*, IV: *Wiedertäuferakten*, 1527-1626 (1951), 181.

26. Of course, extremists of the enthusiastic type were always present, too; mainly in Thuringia where a strong spiritualistic and chiliastic undercurrent in the early 1530s still reflected some influence of Thomas Müntzer. Cf. the story of the Anabaptist Hans Römer prior to 1534; Paul Wappler, *Das Täufertum in Thüringen* (1913), 38-44; also John Oyer, "Anabaptism in Central Germany," *MQR*, XXXV (1961), 25.

27. Cf. Cohn, *The Pursuit of the Millennium*.

28. Cf. Wolfgang Schäufele, *Das missionarische Bewusstsein and Wirken der Täufer, dargestellt nach oberdeutschen Quellen* (1966). Other references are Franklin Littell, *The Anabaptist View of the Church* (sec. ed., 1958), chapter V: "The Great Commission"; Wilhelm Wiswedel's thorough study in *ARG* (1943 and 1948); and Johann Loserth, *Der Communismus der mährischen Wiedertäufer* (1894), 93-97.

29. Robert Friedmann, "Hutterite Book of Medieval Origin," *MQR*, XXX (1956), 65-71.

30. Ernst Benz, *Ecclesia Spiritualis* (1934), 405.

31. Müller, *Glaubenszeugnisse*, 225.

32. Hans J. Hillerbrand, "An Early Anabaptist Treatise on the Christian and the State," *MQR*, XXXII (1958), 28-47, with a facsimile reproduction of the entire pamphlet. See also above, note 8.

33. J. C. Wenger, "The Doctrinal Position of the Swiss Brethren," *MQR*, XXIV (1950), 70.

34. Walther Köhler, "Die Züricher Täufer," in *Gedenkschrift zum 400-jährigen Jubiläum der Taufgesinnten oder Mennoniten* (1925), 48-64, especially p. 61.

35. Köhler used the old Egli edition of 1878. The fine edition by von Muralt and Schmidt, *Quellen zur Geschichte der Täufer in der Schweiz*, I (1952), has an even richer content.

E

Ecclesiology: The Suffering Brotherhood; the Ordinances

The relentless persecution of Anabaptists in Switzerland, Germany, and Austria made the establishment of Anabaptist "churches" most difficult, in fact well-nigh impossible. The

word *Gemeinden* or *Gemeinschaften* would be a more exact
term for these organized brotherhoods, descriptive for both
their worship and brotherly living. Only Moravia, with its con-
ditional toleration, had such brotherhood-churches with elected
preachers and elders and with an adopted church discipline
(*Ordnung*). Otherwise only small groups here and there could
meet in remote places at night to worship together and to
celebrate the Lord's Supper in a simple form. During the
formative years of the movement there was hardly anywhere
a solidly organized congregation of any permanency.

And yet it has been claimed with some justification that
the *idea* of the "church" represents the very center of Anabaptist theology and thinking, and that this was primarily the
point on which Anabaptism and Protestantism separated; and
further that one understands Anabaptism best and most
profoundly when starting with this concept of the brotherhood-
church. This is, for instance, the main thesis of Franklin H.
Littell,[1] who was particularly fascinated by the idea that in
the Anabaptist church he saw the realization of the ideal of
restitution of the primitive or apostolic church.[2] We have
sufficient sources for the study of this remarkable new beginning of a church-type (unknown otherwise, in spite of the
Waldensians, Franciscan Spiritualists, and Bohemian Brethren,
or "Minor Church"). Cornelius Krahn, who studied the theology
of Menno Simons, speaks expressly of his "ecclesiocentric
theology,"[3] meaning that for Menno's thinking the church idea
stood in the very center of all his writings and workings.
Also Harold S. Bender, the expert scholar of the Swiss Brethren, once accepted this claim of the centrality of the church
idea among the Anabaptists, in contrast to the idea of personal
salvation in normative Protestantism. But by 1950, with the
accumulation of new evidence, he recognized that the Anabaptist idea of the church is derivative, based on the deeper
idea of discipleship, which of course also implies an active
covenanting into a brotherhood, without which discipleship
could not be realized.[4]

Nevertheless, few theological topics were more broadly
discussed by the Anabaptists than their "church-idea" or

ecclesiology, even though there is only one full-length Anabaptist tract on the *Gemeinde*, the clear and very spiritual treatise by Dirck Philips, *Van die Ghemeynte Godts* (1560).[5] But whether we study Peter Riedemann's elaborate *Rechenschaft*, or the "Seven Articles of Schleitheim," or Marpeck's writings, or simply the amply assembled records in the *Täuferakten* series, the *Gemeinde* looms large everywhere as one of the most essential elements in Anabaptist thought, and as the very distinguishing mark, setting it apart from the *Volkskirche* of the various establishments.[6] To emphasize this fact in the present context is of some significance inasmuch as Anabaptism also distinguishes itself in this respect very definitely from Spiritualism, which was a close relative in the first decade of the Anabaptist movement. Spiritualists were not really interested in the concreteness of a life in an organized brotherhood. They were satisfied with a "circle" of friends, such as formed, for instance, around Caspar Schwenckfeld. Or they felt the severe loneliness of spiritualistic individualism, as was the case with Sebastian Franck, who felt himself unable to join any type of association. Spiritualists in general had little regard for externals, whether church disciplines or church ordinances or anything not exclusively spirit-bound — in stark contrast to the Anabaptists, for whom such concrete forms of realization were the *sine qua non.*

That Spiritualists preferred to speak of the invisible church is understandable, for a visible church can never completely represent the ideal of the Spiritualists. But even Martin Luther and his fellow theologians likewise taught in principle the "hidden" or invisible church as their very ideal — of which the established state churches were but weak images. The idea of the invisible church originated with Augustine.

For the Anabaptists nothing could be further from the truth than that. *Theirs was always a visible church,* the living brotherhood-congregation which they regarded, at least in part, as the nucleus of God's kingdom on earth or its attempted realization.[7] In this sense Littell speaks correctly of "realized eschatology."[8] A present-day Hutterite preacher in Canada in a conversation with me called the church the "Vorhof zum Paradies" (the anteroom to paradise). If that has been the basic feeling of the brethren, then ideal and reality are not too far apart, and no theology of an "invisible church" could have meaning for them. It is in the present daily life that those islands of peace, unity of the spirit, and true communion (*Gemeinschaft*) are being lived and practiced, as a result of the basic center of Anabaptist theology: the doctrine of the "kingdom of God," and likewise as a result of its opposition to the "kingdom of the devil or prince of darkness."

In this way the external ideal of Anabaptist church life might be circumscribed to some degree. Even though its realization was often prevented by the civil authorities, potentially, at least, the "church" was always present, if only in clandestine celebrations of the breaking of bread and drinking of wine, or by way of itinerant visits among the "family" of brethren. That these churches were always "gathered" churches may almost be taken for granted. But this fact would not be very helpful toward a deeper appreciation of the essence of the Anabaptist church idea. More conducive, perhaps, to that end is Ernst Troeltsch's distinction between "absolute" and "relative" natural law in theology.[9] Practically all the great church bodies in Christendom subscribe to the latter, the relative natural law, accepting compromises with the imperfections of this world and excusing themselves with Adam's Fall, when the absolute natural law was "lost." Anabaptists, however, separated themselves from the "world" exactly by reason of these compromises. Still one may rightly ask whether the "absolute natural law" is really the same as the "commandments of God," and this, whether the Decalogue or the sayings of Jesus. Naturally, by accepting a believer's baptism the Anabaptist became an absolutist in matters of faith, prepared and willing even to die for it. But he did not speculate on natural law (a term of the Stoics) one way or another since it is foreign to the revealed Word of God. Thus, our discussion ends inconclusive, and we might do better to search for new formulations in the quest for a theology of the church among Anabaptists.

The following discussion falls into two clearly separated sec-tions: (a) What is the church as such and how is it constituted; and (b) What are the special functions of the church, "how was this church-idea actualized and maintained?"[10]

(A)

The Church Idea of the Anabaptists and Its Theological Constitution

Nowhere in Anabaptist writings is there any reference to Matthew 16, which in Catholic dogmatics is considered the very foundation stone of the church. Stressing this dominical word, "Thou art Peter and on this rock I will build my church (*ecclesia*)," has a certain legalistic connotation as if saying: here rests my birthright. Anabaptists were children of the Spirit, not of the law, and therefore they had little use for this type of claim. Their reference, at least within the early period of their history, is to the prompting and working of the Spirit in the believers. In this sense Peter Riedemann, the outstanding Hutterite "theologian," may be considered our crown witness as he indulges in a rather outspoken biblical spiritualism. In the section, "What the Church Is," of his *Rechenschaft* of 1541, he has this to say:

> The church is a lantern (*Luzerne*) of righteousness in which the light of grace is borne and held before the whole world. [The church] is completely filled with the light of Christ. Its brightness shines out into the distance to give light to others who are still walking in darkness. Thus whoso-ever endures and suffers the working of the Spirit of Christ is a member of this church. . . . God gathers together. his church through the Spirit, and it is this Spirit of Christ and not man that leads the church."[11]

Here then is the foundation: the possession of the Spirit which transforms the believer into what later was called "a saint." Accordingly, Riedemann says that the church is a "com-

munity of saints"[12] who become "partakers of his grace,"
members of the body of Christ (*corpus Christi* rather than *corpus christianum*) and united with Christ in a *community of
the Spirit* (referring to 1 John 1:3), a "chosen holy nation"
(1 Peter 2:9), as Riedemann quotes at another place.

This description may be further deepened through a
statement by Pilgram Marpeck in his *Verantwortung* of
1545:

> The church of Christ — inwardly of spiritual quality, and
> outwardly as a body before the world — consists of men born
> of God. They bear in their cleansed flesh and blood the
> sonship of God in the *unity of the Holy Spirit [in der
> Einigkeit des Heiligen Geistes]* which has cleansed minds
> and dispositions.[13]

Eberhard Arnold, the founder of the modern Society of Brothers, who in the twentieth century went through experiences
almost identical with those of the Anabaptists of the sixteenth century, expressed nearly the same idea when he called
the *Gemeinde* a community of the "unity of the Spirit
(*Gemeinschaft der Geisteinheit*)."

That seems to be a rather profound and fitting characterization also of the brotherhood-church of the Anabaptists. If
the brothers are all genuine members of the one "body of
Christ," then the "unity of the spirit" is a natural corollary
of this presupposition, and with it goes all the rest: internal peace, brotherly love, cooperation, sharing of material
things, and concern for the preservation of the purity of the
group. That sounds almost too high a goal ever to be
achieved. Yet the original testimonials, mainly up to the years
1550/60, seem to bear out that this ideal was at least
approximated.

Essential for this type of church are two traits: (1) that
no spiritual distinctions were made between lay members and
preachers, for all were of "one priestly nation" (1 Peter
2:5, 9), and (2) that no distinctions were made between secular
and sacred work, the plowing of the fields or assembling for
worship, for all areas of life were in principle sanctified

and transfigured within this church. All of life was one great service of God and surrender to God. Quite appropriate is therefore the observation by a modern author that a brotherhood of this kind may rightly be said to be living in a sort of "heavenly citizenship."[14]

Reducing all these ideas theologically to some basic principles, two stand out: (1) belief in the primacy of the kingdom of God, versus a world of darkness, and belief in the church as an avenue to it;[15] and (2) the soteriological idea that "one cannot come to God except together with one's brother" (see above, Part III, C). Or expressed more figuratively: the vertical relationship "God to man" and the horizontal relationship "brother to brother" are inseparable. The binding together of the brethren is as essential for the disciple as is dedication to obedience to God. For all of this, the apostolic example is usually referred to as normative, summed up in the thesis of a "restitution" of the primitive church.[16]

Some recent attempts of interpretation of the Anabaptist church-idea will now be listed. Franklin Littell lists three "emphases": (a) The eschatological: the Anabaptist church understood in light of a "realized eschatology." This represents the kingdom idea. (b) The covenantal nature of the church: the voluntary congregating of believers into a covenant (*Bund*), an idea dominant with Denck, Hut, and Marpeck, about which more will be said below. (c) The "restitution" principle: The apostolic pattern assumes a normative character.[17]

Franz Heimann, who studied primarily Peter Riedemann and his *Rechenschaft*, proposed a set of three further descriptions:[18] (a) The church as a "lantern of righteousness," which illuminates the world and to which those who have been gathered through the Holy Spirit draw near. (b) The empirical community (*koinonia*), occasionally also identified as the embodiment of the spiritual church of Christ. Here the brotherhood claim of belonging to the true church is not derived from any historical continuity but is based exclusively on spiritual grounds: to be in the church of Christ means to be in the house of the Holy Spirit. The members, a fellowship of committed disciples, thus become torch-bearers, apostles of the light. Furthermore, the church is (c) a fellowship of the Lord's Table (*Abendmahlsgemeinde*). This most seminal idea seems to have originated with Balthasar Hubmaier, mainly in his tract *Eine Form des Nachtmahls Christi* (1527), but Riedemann also integrated it into his own vision of the church.[19] Its corollary is of major significance inasmuch as the unity of such a fellowship has to be in existence *prior* to the actual breaking of bread and drinking of the cup.[20] Heimann reformulated his understanding of these Anabaptist ideas concerning the church thus:[21] first an inner "fellowship of the Lord's Table" is brought about by the spirit of Christ; then the external establishment of community of goods is considered necessary for the perfect realization of the first, the inner aspect; and third, the practice of brotherly discipline together with ban and exclusion is accepted as the only means within a redeemed society by which the intended purity (the "church without spot and wrinkle") can be safeguarded. Legitimately the brethren could here refer to the Lord's injunction in Matthew 18:15-17. To them the ban was nothing but the practice of a form of brotherly love to help the one who went astray to find his way back into the holy community. Discipline assumed a redemptive quality besides its primary cathartic function.

Of course, neither Littell nor Heimann exhausted the possible theological aspects of Anabaptist ecclesiology; some additional points of emphasis will come into focus in this study.

A number of aspects, some mentioned before and others still to be formulated, will now be given consideration. There is first of all the idea of *the church as a visible covenantal community:* it is an idea set forth by Hans Denck, Hans Hut, and his followers, and Pilgram Marpeck. One of its most concise formulations we find in the "Sieben Urteile" (Seven Decisions) of 1527. These seven theses presumably originated with Hans Hut,[22] one of the most creative and profound spirits of South German Anabaptism. The only full exposition of them is found in a confession of faith by Ambrosius Spittelmaier in 1527,[23] in which this noble follower of Hut slightly changed and enriched his teacher's theses. Article One deals with the divine covenant and reads in part as follows: "We are to covenant ourselves to God to remain with Him in one love, one spirit, one faith, and one baptism (Ephesians 4:5). On the other hand God covenants (binds Himself) to be our Father and to stay with us in tribulation." [24]

J. C. Wenger discusses the wide ramifications of this basic concept of covenant (*Bund*), [25] which became dominant both among the South German Anabaptists and the early Dutch Melchiorites, the forerunners of the Doopsgezinden. Pilgram Marpeck too liked to call his fellow Anabaptists *Bundesgenossen* or covenanters, and his first large book, the *Vermahnung* of 1542, says in its title expressly: "Bericht zu warer Christlichen pundtsvereynigung aller waren glaubigen . . . zu hilff und trost," etc., thus indicating that also to him the church was essentially a covenantal association or brotherhood. [26]

To Ambrosius Spittelmaier as to most early Anabaptists the church was essentially a *sharing brotherhood*. [27] Where there is perfect brotherly love (as it is supposed to be in the authentic "body of Christ"), the idea of private property vanishes in one way or another. Hence one practices either a communism of love (Troeltsch), which denotes a concern for the needy; or full community of goods as in the Moravian experiment among the Hutterites, Philippites, and Gabrielites. Article Two of Hut's "Seven Decisions" of 1527 [28] reads in part as follows:

> Nobody can inherit the kingdom of God unless he is poor with Christ, for a Christian has nothing of his own, no place where he can lay his head. . . . A Christian should have all things in common with his brother, that is, not allow him to suffer need. . . . For a Christian looks more to his neighbor than to himself.

In this neither Hans Hut nor his follower Ambrosius Spittelmaier stood alone. Actually, ever since Hubmaier, this idea of the "communism" of love as an essential feature of the true

church had been a fairly general conviction of all Anabaptists
of the formative years and was realized to a large extent also
outside Moravia.

Hubmaier has one significant paragraph on this subject
in his *Gespräch auf Zwinglis Taufbüchlein* (1525/26):

> That a man should always have a concern for his fellow;
> that the hungry be fed, the thirsty receive drink, and the
> naked be clothed. For no one is master of his own goods
> but only their steward (*Schaffner*) and distributer(*Austeiler*).
> Certainly there is no one who would say that one should
> take away what belongs to the other and distribute it
> (*gemein machen*). Rather one should leave the cloak along
> with the coat.[29]

Even more outspoken are testimonies by Hans Hut,[30]
Leonhard Schiemer,[31] Hans Schlaffer,[32] Wolfgang Brandhuber,[33] and some eight years later by Ulrich Stadler,[34] not
to mention the Hutterites. They all indicate the same
orientation. But rarely do we find the radicalism of Spittelmaier's words, which perhaps correspond most nearly to the
Franciscan ideal of apostolic poverty.

In an earlier study, trying to understand the deeper arguments of the doctrine of communal life with the Anabaptist idea of the church, I found principally three motives:[35]
(a) Brotherly love in action, a longing for sharing and
togetherness with the brother in Christ. "Wo keine Gemeinschaft ist," they would say, "da ist auch keine rechte Liebe
(where there is no community, there is also no genuine
love)."[36] (b) *Gelassenheit*, yieldedness or resignation to the
will of God, and renunciation of any form of selfishness, and
(c) obedience to the divine commands. As one gives up his
own will, he naturally accepts God's commands as the basis
and guideposts for action. "It is only through communal living that the blood of Christ may cleanse sinful men." Heimann is right in calling this form of living a "theocratic
communism." Thus it is clear that the church of the Anabaptists had nothing in it of an institutional character. It was all
life and realization — an "embodiment" of supreme ideas,

above all, of the idea of the kingdom of God, foreshadowed in the brotherhood here and now.

The next problem to be considered concerns the *inner dynamics* of such a brotherhood-church, the well nigh impossibility of realizing in the historical concreteness an ideal as sublime as the kingdom of God — or the "church without spot or wrinkle." As has already been emphasized: the Anabaptists never taught perfectionism.[37] They knew only too well that few persons would ever be able to live on a summit all their lives. Backsliding and offending the group would necessarily occur time and again. For that reason the ban or "exclusion" has been an integral part of such a church, an act of brotherly love to assist the failing member in his struggle for the right path. Without the ban,[38] that is, without the supervision of the inner purity of the church by appointed and usually charismatic overseers, there could never be an effective fellowship of the Lord's Table. We are inclined to call this problem — a basic one in every idea of the church — the "inner dynamics" of church life.[39] Dynamics it certainly is, and as we speak of Anabaptism as a form of existential Christianity, it would not be out of place to coin the term "existential dynamics." Roughly it follows this scheme:

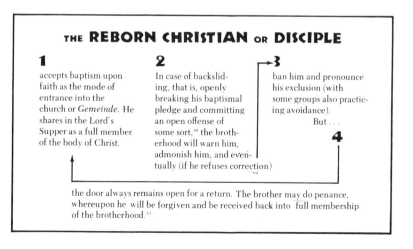

THE **REBORN CHRISTIAN** OR **DISCIPLE**

1
accepts baptism upon faith as the mode of entrance into the church or *Gemeinde*. He shares in the Lord's Supper as a full member of the body of Christ.

2
In case of backsliding, that is, openly breaking his baptismal pledge and committing an open offense of some sort,[40] the brotherhood will warn him, admonish him, and eventually (if he refuses correction)

3
ban him and pronounce his exclusion (with some groups also practicing avoidance).
But . . .

4

the door always remains open for a return. The brother may do penance, whereupon he will be forgiven and be received back into full membership of the brotherhood.[41]

Surveying this inner dynamics of the church, we easily
recognize a shift in character. As a "lantern of righteousness"
or "covenantal community (*Koinonia*)," as a "fellowship of the
Lord's Table," or as the "body of Christ," the church on-
tologically understands itself to be the nucleus of the kingdom,
with all its intended perfection. As a human establishment,
however, we also see the church coping with shortcomings
and tensions of all sorts. Instead of unity the brotherhoods
passed through divisions and strife, and were eventually
to experience even a loss of the incipient spirit. Thus, discipline, including the ban, became a necessity for bringing
the realities more in line with the ideal.

In this connection it appears quite helpful to call the
Anabaptist brotherhood a *church of order*, as, for instance,
Harold S. Bender had done.[42] For in it the corporate body
determines in principle the pattern of life for its members
and assumes the final authority over their behavior. The individual person, however, submits to this ruling freely at the
time of his baptismal pledge. The outward expression
of such an "order" is a document usually called "Church
Discipline" (*Ordnung der Gemeinde*). In Anabaptism a number
of such documents are known which in their strictness and
comprehensiveness distinctly differentiate themselves from the
church disciplines of the large established church bodies. In
some way they are reminiscent of the *regulae* of medieval
monastic orders. They either represent a sort of constitution
of a particular brotherhood group, thus establishing that
group, or a codification of already existing orders and practices, in this way establishing a firm tradition for future
generations.

The oldest of these documents originated with the first
Anabaptist congregation in Bern, Switzerland, dated not later
than 1526/27. It is a rather brief document which has surprisingly escaped scholarly attention until recently.[43] Obviously it established that group as a corporate entity, and
it expresses the genius of early Anabaptism very well. It
may best be discussed together with the second oldest
Anabaptist discipline, the *Ordnung der Gemein*, written by

Leonhard Schiemer, a follower of Hans Hut, while in prison in Rattenberg, Tyrol, in December 1527 and January 1528, facing ultimate martyrdom.[44] Its subtitle reads characteristically, "How a Christian Is to Live." It was drawn up out of a deep concern for the spiritual welfare of the small but strong brotherhood at that mining city of the Inn Valley.[45] Schiemer felt himself to be the responsible shepherd of that new congregation. Not unfittingly it was called a "prophetic" church discipline.

The Bernese discipline has seven articles, the Rattenberg document twelve, but by and large they have the same content. They rule that the brethren should assemble frequently, if possible three or four times a week, and the first point of order was to be a mutual exhortation (*Vermahnung*) to remain steadfast in their faith, considering the hostility of their surrounding. They should be conscientiously instructed by one responsible brother who would exposit the Holy Scriptures to them. Stress is laid on proper behavior so that they would not give offense to the "world outside." Cursing and vulgar language are forbidden. Any break in these regulations is to be punished according to Matthew 18, as the purity of the group is a paramount principle.

Both documents contain an article concerning sharing, that is, the requirement of some form of a primitive "communism of love." "All things should be held in common," expressing the concern that needy brethren must not suffer while others have enough. Regulations are also set up concerning the frequent celebration of the Lord's Supper which is thought of as an expression of genuine brotherly togetherness. A vital concomitant to the Lord's Supper, also underscoring such togetherness, is the regularly practiced brotherly meal. But here, too, great moderation is enjoined. The Rattenberg document adds that "a Christian must always be prepared for the cross," a point ordinarily not found in a church regulation but most natural in the situation prevailing in Tyrol in 1527. The Bernese document has no such reference to the cross, thus indicating that it must have been drawn up prior to the time when, later in 1527, persecution began in that city. The

Tyrolean discipline finally reminds the brethren that "we should watch always and expect the coming of the Lord," perhaps an echo of the teachings of Hans Hut.

Both of these brief documents have the character of a "constitution" establishing "order" among those who have covenanted in their newly won faith. In this both have the ring of an existential concreteness which is a far cry from any "legal"-type document as was generally found in the disciplines of the large territorial churches of the sixteenth century.

It is characteristic for all early Anabaptist confessions of faith to be basically — their doctrinal content aside — nothing but such church regulations or disciplines. This applies equally to the Schleitheim Articles of 1527 and the *Rechenschaft* of Peter Riedemann, which are otherwise quite different. The Schleitheim document, to which Michael Sattler gave the title: *Vereinigung etzlicher Kinder Gottes,*[46] deals exclusively with those articles upon which a union or agreement of all like-minded individuals and groups was made possible. Thus it assumed the character of a constitution and belongs rightly at the beginning of that great venture.

Swiss Anabaptism formally began with the first adult baptism in Zurich on January 21, 1525. It was only two years later, on February 24, 1527, that a number of brethren assembled at Schleitheim to discuss and draw up such a document which in due time became "normative" at least for all the Swiss Brethren. The seven articles concern (1) baptism; (2) the ban; (3) the Lord's Supper; (4) separation from the world; (5) the office of shepherd; (6) the sword, that is, the relationship to civil authorities; and (7) the taking of an oath, forbidden for a disciple. On all these points consensus was sought and given, for it was a voluntarily accepted *regula,* rather than a law dictated from above. Discipline according to Matthew 18 was one of the major duties of the shepherds of the group who had to supervise the purity of their church. If banning should become necessary it ought to be done prior to the "breaking of bread" so that the fellowship of the Lord's Table would remain a gathering of genuine disciples, a foreshadowing of the eternal kingdom.

Riedemann's *Rechenschaft* was intended in part to inform the Landgrave Philipp of Hesse about the content of the Anabaptist faith, and in part to give the brethren at home in Moravia a clear and scriptural formulation of what they believed.[47] Customarily it has been classified as a "confession of faith," as the title indicates: "Account of our Religion, Doctrine, and Faith." But a closer look soon reveals this bulky document[48] to be a sort of "codification" of already prevailing practices and traditions of the previous ten or eleven years. Thus it may find its proper evaluation within the context of the present chapter on church discipline. The first section of this amazing document deals with the Apostles' Creed and other articles belonging to a confession of faith. The next section treats the idea of the church, together with baptism, the Lord's Supper, and church offices.

Finally the large concluding section provides the regulations of the more practical aspects of brotherhood life, explaining "how we live." It contains chapters on marriage, community of goods, general behavior (including the prohibition of oath-taking, soldiering, innkeeping, and even trading). At the end of this section the chapters on the ban and readmission strangely deemphasize these points. Around 1545, it was printed in Moravia in a small edition as a pocket book, and in 1565 a second edition was printed there. It is still in use with the Hutterite Brethren in North America and has been reprinted by them as late as 1962. That it became the standard work of the Hutterites can easily be appreciated because of its comprehensiveness and fair balance. It is well founded on biblical grounds and its margins contain close to three thousand Bible references. In a sense it may be considered fairly representative of the Anabaptist genius.

The last example of such church regulations in sixteenth-century Anabaptism is a document of a slightly different genius: Leupold Scharnschlager's *Gemeinsame Ordnung der Glieder Christi, in sieben Artikeln gestellt*, of about 1540.[49] Scharnschlager is known as the most alert co-worker of Pilgram Marpeck, and the *Ordnung* belongs to his circle.

But an unsettling question arises at once: For whom did he draw up such an "Order of the members of Christ"? Except for small groups here and there in Alsace and one colony in Moravia, the Marpeck brotherhood did not really exist as a corporate body or "church." It is not known that Scharn-schlager ever shepherded any one of these scattered congregations; around 1540 he seems to have lived in the neighborhood of Augsburg. Thus we probably have here a church regulation for the diaspora of the Marpeck followers. Accordingly, the document is somewhat vague and surprisingly mild, as Scharnschlager had really not too much charismatic authority to legislate for any group. And yet the need was felt, and the document was compiled to instruct fellow believers about basic principles normative for the "body of Christ" anywhere. Interestingly, it mentions the advisability of "community of goods," referring not only to apostolic example, but also to Paul's epistles such as Romans 15:25 f.; 1 Corinthians 16:1 ff.; and 2 Corinthians 9:1 f. In dealing with the ban it understandably counsels gentleness lest the spirit of love be violated. Of all the early Anabaptist church orders known, this is obviously the weakest one. Twenty years later the Marpeck group disappeared, more or less fusing with the Swiss Brethren in South Germany, except for Moravia where a small congregation persisted. The document survived in one codex only, the recently discovered *Kunstbuch* of 1561.[50]

Our discussion of Anabaptist ecclesiology would still be incomplete without our touching upon two more points not strictly theological in nature: (1) the idea of the "suffering church" or the "church under the cross" and (2) the idea of voluntaryism in the Anabaptist brotherhood-church, another term for the principle of liberty of conscience.

Ethelbert Stauffer's "theology of martyrdom"[51] underscores a basic outlook within Anabaptism concerning the function of the church of Christ in this world. Being both a leaven and a challenge, this church will inescapably incur persecution by the world, resulting in the suffering and death of its members. Stauffer collected voluminous material to substantiate the spirit of martyrdom as constitutive for the disciple and his church. The first document in this direction is Conrad Grebel's famous epistle to Thomas Müntzer of September 5, 1524, antedating the earliest adult baptism by four and a half months. In this letter Grebel says:

> True Christian believers are sheep among wolves, sheep for the slaughter. They must be baptized in anguish and affliction, tribulation, persecution, suffering and death. They must be tried with fire. . . . And if you must suffer for it, you know well that it cannot be otherwise. Christ must suffer still more in his members.[52]

Harold S. Bender, who wrote the definitive biography of Conrad Grebel, made this idea of the "suffering church" a real cornerstone of the incipient Anabaptist movement. And certainly every catechumen instructed for baptism was assiduously forewarned about the tremendous risk involved in this step.

But what does this have to do with the "church" as a corporate body? To answer the question a subtle distinction must be made between two great and similar-sounding ideas: on the one hand we encounter the "theology of the cross" (*Kreuzestheologie*), a term introduced by Thomas Müntzer but subsequently also much used in Lutheranism, while on the other hand we meet the "theology of martyrdom" of the Anabaptists, the idea of the suffering church. The "theology of the cross" seems to be understood as an affair of each single believer individually, having to do with profound personal dilemmas such as *Anfechtung*, that is, inner doubt, uncertainty, even despair, and the like, which would undermine one's faith and produce the feeling of anxiety. In our era the same idea is sometimes called "Christian existence today." It means a dilemma between our longing for faith and certitude of salvation, and our inner difficulties in attaining genuine faith. John H. Yoder aptly calls it the "Heilsweg eines Menschen in Anfechtung" (literally, the "salvation-path of a person in despair").[53]

The other idea, sounding so similar to the "theology of the cross," yet so vastly different, is the "theology of martyrdom," born of an imperturbable faith in its encounter with the "world." Here it is the antagonistic world which attempts to crush this faith, in whatever form it tries to become realized. The theme here is not the inner conflict of the single believer (although such conflicts abound here, too) but the conflict of the brotherhood as a collective whole, unavoidably exposed to suffering in the world, yet willing to endure it for the sake of the kingdom. For, as the Apostle Paul said, "We must through much tribulation enter into the kingdom of God" (Acts 14:22). A good illustration of this idea is the dramatic story of the Hutterites during the 1540s when the entire group was expelled from Moravia, Hungary, and Austria, eventually digging underground tunnels[54] in order to survive somehow as a collective whole. "We turned hither and thither," they wrote, "and did not know what to do next." But they stayed together, nevertheless, and did not disperse; eventually they were able to return to their Bruderhof. Scenes like this have been repeated many times up to the present. It just could not be otherwise according to their basic Christian dualism, since "kingdom of God" and "world" simply do not agree. "The true church of Christ," Menno Simons wrote, "has this characteristic whereby it is recognizable as the true church of Christ, that it suffers persecution but does not persecute."[55]

The last point of this first part of ecclesiology is the issue of "liberty of conscience" within this church and the basic principle of voluntaryism.[56] The Anabaptist church is a "gathered" church, an association freely accepted and freely joined with; no compulsion or external influence is admitted to interfere with the freedom of the baptismal pledge. And should it happen that one partner in a marriage becomes a member of that church while the other remains outside, the situation has to be accepted and no effort is to be made to change it by any form of compulsion. And even afterward, when a person has already accepted the new path, his conscience will still remain his final authority on whether or not he feels called to fill his place in the oneness of the Spirit.

In fact, Anabaptism was the earliest champion of liberty of conscience in the face of the gross intolerance of the established churches everywhere. "Christ's people are a free, unforced, and uncompelled people, who receive Christ with desire and a willing heart,"[57] wrote Kilian Auerbacher of Moravia to Martin Bucer in 1534. Hence "faith is not to be compelled but is to be accepted as a [free] gift of God."[58] Nothing could be further from Anabaptist thinking than compulsion of any sort in matters of faith, for coercion would destroy that "unity of the spirit" and render the Anabaptist way meaningless. But it also needs to be stressed that the "philosophy" and motives of Anabaptism were certainly radically different from those of contemporary champions of religious toleration. These were Humanists, such as for instance, Sebastian Castellio, who fought a war for "toleration," the end result of which was John Locke and the Toleration Act of 1689. These humanistic struggles had to do with the triumph of reason over beliefs, hence meant basically indifference to the spectrum of churches and their creeds. It is clear that nothing of that kind applies to the Radical Reformation. Its representatives surely were absolutists, and "toleration" was not a word in their vocabulary. But they were respecters of the Spirit of which the gospel says that "the wind bloweth where it listeth." Only out of this lofty vision were these people ready to defend the principle of voluntaryism; combined, however, as always with another principle, namely that of discipline. The latter would exclude too much arbitrariness among the individual members, while the former would emphasize that their church was in the last analysis the church of the Spirit and a "lantern of righteousness."

(B)

The Special Functions of the Church: The Way in Which the Church Is Actualized and Maintained

In the last section of this study belongs first and foremost a discussion of the theology of the two ordinances, baptism and the Lord's Supper, as understood by early Anabaptism. In addition three other functions must be considered: (a) the ban, as the prerogative of the autonomous *Gemeinde* to watch over its inner purity; (b) the teaching-commission of the church, including worship and preaching the divine Word; and finally (c) the outreach, mission, and "proselytizing" wherever the German tongue was understood.

(1) Baptismal Theology[59]

The main biblical locus quoted by Anabaptists when discussing baptism is 1 Peter 3:21, in Luther's translation: "Baptism is a covenant [*Bund*] of a good conscience with God." Hans Denck seems to have been the first to point to this passage. But there is some question as to whether the translation of this verse in Luther's Bible is correct. Does the Greek original really speak of a covenant? The Greek word ἐπερώτημα, here rendered as *Bund*, poses difficulties in translation. "Pledge" would perhaps be appropriate, though strangely enough is never used by Bible translators. The Zurich Bible has *Kundschaft*, and this term was also used by Hubmaier, for which reason he knows of no "covenantal theology of baptism." Marpeck discussed this question of proper translation at some length in the *Verantwortung*,[60] but in the *Vermahnung* a few years earlier, he too speaks of *Bund* or *Verpündtnuss* in the context of baptism.[61]

Other loci, less often used for theological speculations, are Titus 3:5, reading in Luther's translation: "Baptism is the bath of regeneration,"[62] and (at least with Hans Hut) Revelation 7:3, which calls baptism "a seal on the forehead" . . . for those who will not be hurt by the catastrophe of the end-

time. Here baptism assumes a clearly eschatological connotation, typical of Hans Hut and his followers. Another term
used in connection with baptism when understood as a pledge
or vow to discipleship, somewhat comparable to monastic
vows, is *Versieglung* (sealing), very popular with Hans Hut,
the Hutterites, and Pilgram Marpeck. "Baptism is the sealing
of the new life," soon became a standard phrase. Marpeck
even found that this idea goes back to no less a person
than Tertullian (c. AD 200). "Tertullian," he writes,[63] "said
in the 'Book of Repentance' that this bath is a sealing of
faith." And finally the term *Verwilligung*[64] is frequently used
in connection with baptism upon faith, primarily by Hans
Hut in his profound tract *Vom Geheimnus der Tauff* (1527),
where he says,[65] "Accept the sign of baptism for a covenant
of consent before a Christian church," or again, "Baptism is
a sign, a covenant, a parable, and a reminder of the consent,
bringing to mind what such a person has to expect through
right baptism" (namely suffering).[66]

Thus adult baptism was considered more than just a ritual
(what it was almost bound to become for the third and the
following generations where the young folk simply went through
a routine to perpetuate the church). In the beginning it
definitely assumed an existential, and with Hut also an
eschatological character, a decision for life. The standard
term throughout our sources remains "Bund," which justifies
our speaking generally of an Anabaptist "covenantal baptismal
theology" (Rollin S. Armour).

A covenant is a pledge which in Anabaptist thinking works
in three directions: (a) a covenant between God and man;
(b) one between man and God; and (c) also one between
man and man, thus establishing the church or *Gemeinde*.[67]
By accepting baptism the believer, a disciple of Christ, now
enters the brotherhood as an equal to other members, or more
specifically as member of the spiritual "body of Christ," a
quality shared with all other members.

In Marpeck's language baptism also means *Mitzeugnis*,[68]
a term not easily translated. Usually it is rendered as co-
witnessing, but "attestation" is nearer to the original mean-

ing. Baptism then is the external attestation for the internally
experienced new birth. The external act therefore works in
two directions: (1) for the incorporation (*Einverleibung*) of the
catechumen into the covenant with God, and (2) at the same
time for his incorporation into God's holy church.[69] In this
sense baptism is far more than a mere sign. It has a testimonial quality, *the attestation for a previously experienced
"baptism" with the Holy Spirit.* There can be no question
that in the early period of Anabaptism adult baptism had this
profound spiritual connotation.

This becomes particularly clear in the threefold distinction made by early Anabaptist authors when speaking of
baptism. In this they follow a suggestion in 1 John 5:6-8,
even though baptism is not discussed there. Anabaptist
tracts time and again speak of a threefold baptism: (a) first and
foremost is the baptism by the Spirit, (b) then follows baptism
with water, and finally (c) the gruesome baptism with blood or
fire. Hubmaier in his treatise *Von dem christlichen Tauff der
Gläubigen* (1525), perhaps his finest monograph, says that
baptism with water serves for renewal of life inasmuch as the
reborn one accepts baptism with water as a testimony of
his innermost spiritual faith.[70] And then he adds significantly: "Baptism does not cleanse the soul, rather it has to be preceded by a 'good conscience' toward God (*mit Gott*) in his inner faith."[71] This quasi-spiritualistic theology totally pre-
cludes any ritualistic interpretation of this act of baptism.

Most outspoken on the subject are two early tracts: Hans
Hut's *Vom Geheimnus der Tauff* (1527) and Leonhard Schiemer's *Von dreyerley Tauff im Neuen Testament* (also 1527).
According to Hut true justification comes only through suffering. No one can escape this "hell," but the believer will
emerge from it, cleansed. For God saves man from all his
tribulations (*Trübsal*) through the "bath of regeneration" (Titus
3:7).[72] Both Hut and Schiemer then elaborate on this new
understanding of "threefold baptism."[73] To it Hut adds
another aspect, the eschatological one, namely that baptism
means also (symbolically) the "entrance ticket into the world to
come," an idea which, however, did not find much response

among fellow Anabaptists.

Baptism, to Hans Hut, implies an ever-readiness to participate in the suffering of Christ. This is understood in a twofold way: (a) as physical suffering in martyrdom, which will always be preceded by (b) "mystical suffering"; that is, man's never-ending struggle with sin. In this context Hut says with profound insight that "true baptism is nothing but a fight with sin throughout life."[74] He explains this by saying that "the water which enters the soul is *Anfechtung,* sadness, anxiety, trembling, and tribulation. Hence baptism always means suffering." Is this whole idea perhaps an echo of Thomas Müntzer who in his *Protestation und Entbietung* of 1524 likewise testified to this inner tribulation and anguish?[75] But then Hut adds significantly: "Baptism is a struggle with sin, mortifying it throughout life."[76]

Leonhard Schiemer adds two more ideas to this new aspect of baptism: one of these is that only a person who himself has turned to Christ in this radical way is empowered or authorized to baptize others. "Hence no one may receive me as a Christian who has not become a Christian himself previously."[77] And then he elaborates still more outspokenly on this point by writing: "Baptism must be administered not by a Jew, a Turk, or pagan but alone by those who have been elected by Christ to this office."[78] It seems that here a quasi-sacramental quality is introduced out of the depth of a charismatic interpretation of this act. Baptism is consequently not only surrender of the self, but also sanctification and reception of the disciple into the "community of saints."

The other pertinent passage is as follows:

In summa: Baptism with water is a confirmation of the inner covenant with God. This might be compared to a man who writes a letter and then asks that it be sealed. But nobody gives his seal or testimonial unless he knows the contents of the letter. Whoever baptizes a child seals an empty letter.[79]

It can be easily understood how arguments of this kind convinced even the unsophisticated man of the correctness of believer's baptism.

In baptism, all these early Anabaptists, and also Marpeck, believed that one has to distinguish between sign and essence (*Zeichen* and *Wesen*). The sign is external, the pouring of water over the recipient, symbolizing the man's own decision and sealing his determination for the new life and the narrow path. The essence, however, lies deeper and concerns the inner surrender of one's self-will to the obedience to God, a spiritual transformation and regeneration which demands the outer sign. This is, incidentally, one of the traits which separated the Anabaptists from the radical spiritualists. For the latter knew no "sign," no real brotherhood, no challenge of tradition, and accordingly their impact upon the world was not felt as a provocative force causing a reaction by government and the world at large.

Baptism with the Spirit was indeed known also to the spiritualists including Thomas Müntzer (who was actually closer to mysticism than to spiritualism). Baptism with water was accepted also by Hans Denck, in spite of his leaning toward spiritualism. Baptism with blood and fire, however, was taught by the Anabaptists only, first by Hubmaier and Hut, but also by Grebel and Sattler and the Swiss Brethren. Baptism with the Spirit was recognized as a gift of salvation which gives power for the new life. Baptism with water works toward the establishment of a church (*Gemeinde*). But the baptism with blood or fire is the final cleansing from sin, according to Anabaptist teaching. For they knew that the tribulation of martyrdom leaves no room for the temptations of sin (compare 1 Peter 4:1).[80] It signifies a situation which is to be appreciated mainly from an eschatological aspect: i.e., as the birth pangs of the kingdom of God which has drawn near and might break in at any moment.

This is, in the briefest outline, the Anabaptist theology of baptism prior to its becoming more routine or traditional.

(2) *The Theology of the Lord's Supper*[81]

That the Anabaptists were given to a so-called rationalistic interpretation of the Lord's Supper, rejecting any supposition of a spiritual presence of Christ in the elements of bread and wine, goes almost without saying. To them neither transubstantiation nor consubstantiation conveyed any meaning. In fact, they even ridiculed such ideas, as Peter Walpot, for instance, did in his Article Book of 1577.[82] In this regard the Anabaptists seem to have mirrored Zwingli's view, understanding the Lord's Supper mainly as a memorial (*Gedächtnismal*) of Christ's supreme sacrifice, and granting to it a symbolic or figurative meaning only. But if it were only this and nothing more it would lack an existential quality and could have easily been discarded altogether as was the case with the radical spiritualists.

Actually, the assembling and the breaking of bread and drinking of wine meant a great deal to the brethren. Otherwise they would not have risked their clandestine celebrations even at night in remote places, forest glens or abandoned mills, for this express purpose. This eating and drinking in brotherly fellowship gave them strength and encouragement and the certitude of belonging to a company of redeemed souls, and of being part of the "true body of Christ."[83] Here a new rich symbolism was developed, different from and beyond the Zwinglian interpretation, a symbolism which, one may safely say, goes back to apostolic, and even pre-apostolic times.

In this regard the research of the outstanding German historian of religion Rudolf Otto may provide helpful insights. In his book, *The Kingdom of God and the Son of Man*,[84] which describes the spiritual elements within the Gospels, we find many surprising parallels to Anabaptist records, making the study of this volume particularly exciting. "Today," he writes, "we often emphasize unduly the means (forgiveness, expiation of sin) over against the purpose, the kingdom of God."[85] And further: "The Lord's Supper was originally thought of as a fraternal meal, a *cheber*, with the intention of consecration."[86] Its prime meaning was no doubt eschatological[87] — consider for instance Luke 22:30 — the feeling prevailed that "the kingdom of God is at hand as the inbreaking power of the transcendent. Christ is himself part of the inbreaking miracle of the eschatological order itself."[88]

Exactly the same spirit prompted Anabaptists to gather and celebrate this fraternal meal. They did not call it a "love feast" but in essence it was one, nevertheless. Such a profound symbol of brotherly unity and togetherness provided a foretaste of the kingdom of God in the here and now, or — to speak with Rudolf Otto — of the inbreaking of a new transcendent reality. In this very real sense the Lord's Supper was more than *only* a memorial. In discussing the Anabaptist church idea, we spoke of it as a "community of the unity of the spirit" and a "fellowship at the Lord's table." This meal then was a confirmation of that inner unity (also called "the body of Christ") and gave the Lord's table the meaning of spiritual sharing and togetherness, the horizontal element in the Anabaptist church idea, which was initially missing in the Zwinglian understanding.

To illustrate this rather existential interpretation of the coming-together and eating and drinking, a parable was popular among the Anabaptists which should interpret this unique fusion of like-minded people into one body, ready to surrender all self-will and to suffer for the sake of the kingdom. It is a parable originating with the Apostolic Age itself, for it is found in the *Didache*, or "The Teachings of the Twelve Apostles." The parable seems to have been popular in the sixteenth century, as it was also known to Luther (1519) and others.[89] Perhaps its earliest documentation among Anabaptists is found in Hans Nadler's deposition at his trial in 1529, referring to the days which he spent in company with Hans Hut in 1526 and 1527. This is what Nadler had to say:

Then we celebrated the Lord's Supper at Augsburg in 1527, the Lord's wine and bread. With the bread the unity among brethren is symbolized. Where there are many small kernels of grain to be combined into one loaf there is need first to grind them and to make them into one flour . . . which can be achieved only through suffering. Just as Christ, our dear Lord, went before us, so too we want to follow him in like manner. And the bread symbolizes the unity of the brotherhood.

Likewise with the wine: many small grapes come together to make the one wine. That happens by means of the press, understood here as suffering. (*Es zeigt uns das Leiden an.*) And thus also the wine indicates suffering. Hence, whoever wants to be in brotherly union, has to drink from the cup of the Lord, for this cup symbolizes suffering.[90]

It appears that it was not Nadler but Hut himself who introduced this parable into Anabaptism, as he introduced so many other new ideas, having been the truly seminal spirit of Anabaptism in South Germany. One should, however, not forget that by 1527 no real *Gemeinde* existed anywhere. There were brethren and sisters here and there, particularly in and around Augsburg and later Strassburg, who met occasionally for such a fellowship meal. But it was a precarious affair which only too often ended in arrest and execution. Thus the meal was really a parallel to the first Supper preceding Calvary, and its symbolism was slanted toward suffering. It is interesting that Peter Riedemann in his first (Gmundener) *Rechenschaft* (1530-31, at which time he was a leader of the Upper-Austrian Anabaptists, and not yet a Hutterite) repeats this parable with exactly the same symbolic meaning. Had he learned it from Hans Hut, or a Hut disciple in Steyr, Linz, or elsewhere; perhaps from the "bishop" of the Upper-Austrian Anabaptists, Wolfgang Brandhuber (martyred in 1529)? We do not know. But the Hut tradition certainly lingered on in that area. Also Pilgram Marpeck included it in his *Vermahnung* of 1542.[91] And in the North, Menno Simons taught almost the same idea, although we do not know his sources:[92]

Just as natural bread has to be kneaded of many kernels of grain broken in the mill, together with water and then baked by the heat of the fire, in the same way the church of Christ is made up of many believers, broken in their hearts by the mill of God's word, baptized with water of the Holy Spirit, and brought together into one body by pure and unadulterated love [at the Lord's Table].[93]

Also within the Hutterite communities this parable of the kernels and grapes is still quoted, but with a new slant. For

it is also applied as an illustration for complete community of
goods. In fact, the parable is often considered one of the
strongest suggestions for this Hutterite idea. The Confession of
Faith of Claus Felbinger, drawn up while in jail in Landshut,
Bavaria, in 1560, includes the parable:

> We also know, praise be to God, the interpretation of this
> high mystery which He wanted to disclose to His loved ones
> in this comforting supper, namely, by means of bread and
> wine He has shown the community of His body. Even as na-
> tural bread is composed by the coming together of many
> grains, ground under the millstones, and each giving the
> others all it possesses, they have community one with an-
> other, and thus become one loaf. And, likewise, as the wine
> is composed of many grapes, each sharing its juice with the
> rest in the wine press, so that they become one drink, even
> so are we also, in that we become completely of one nature
> with Him in life and death, and are all one in Christ. He is
> the vine and we His branches, He the head and we His
> members.[94]

The same idea was expressed twice by the outstanding
Hutterite bishop Peter Walpot: once in his "Epistle to the Swiss
Brethren at Modenbach on the Rhine," in 1577, explaining
to them the idea of community of goods as a divinely
established way of life; and a second time in his "Article Book"
of 1577, where he uses this parable as an illustration in the
third article, "Concerning True Surrender and Christian Community of Goods."[95] The use of this parable may also be
found in the renowned *Sendbrief* of 1650 by the great Hutterite bishop Andreas Ehrenpreis. As the text is slightly
different from all previous examples, we shall quote it too, in
order to make the point still clearer:

> The grains had to be brought together into one flour and
> one loaf. Not one of them could preserve itself as it was, or
> keep what it had. Every grain has given itself and its whole
> strength into the bread. In the same way the grapes. The
> grapes must be pressed for the wine. Every grape gives all
> its strength and all its juice into the uniform wine. In it no
> grape can keep anything for itself. Only in this way does

wine come into being. Grapes and grains which remain whole
are only fit for the pigs or the muck heap. They have nothing to do with bread and wine. If they kept back strength
and body for themselves, they lost everything and remained
lost.[96]

Whether or not this may be called a "theology of the
Lord's Supper" remains a moot question. Essentially it is a
symbolic interpretation to make the celebration of this meal
more meaningful to the brethren in their tense and grim situation. It also fitted their idea of reestablishment of the
apostolic pattern of solemn togetherness, a covenanting that is
pregnant with meaning and expectation. "Where two or three
are assembled in my name," Jesus said, "there I will be, too."
That is how the church actually functioned, an ever-renewing
nucleus of the kingdom of God, symbolically perpetuated by
the two ordinances of baptism and the Lord's Supper.

———

This study of the way in which the church idea was
actualized and *maintained* by the brethren on completely voluntary foundations will be concluded by some further analyses
of functions both theological and practical which are part and
parcel of this church idea. Three points are to be considered
here: (a) The inner discipline of the church, mainly the practice of the ban and excommunication, established upon the
injunction of Jesus to maintain the purity of the group. (b)
The teaching office of the church, that is its observance of Bible studies, catechetical instructions for baptismal candidates,
and the preaching of the Word of God as often as possible.
(c) And finally, the outreach, that is, mission and "proselytizing" throughout the German-speaking areas of Europe. All
of these points have been touched on but need more de-
tailed discussion.

(1) *The Ban*

In the ancient church the ban was considered the third sacrament besides baptism and the Lord's Supper. And indeed, it has this character of an ordinance if one thinks of the injunctions of Jesus in Matthew 18:15-19 (called by the Anabaptists "the rule of Christ") or His pronouncement in Matthew 16 concerning the "power of the two keys." Obviously there can be no genuine purity of the church without strict discipline, voluntarily accepted, to be sure, by all its members. It belongs to the tradition of all nonconformist churches through the ages. Authentic discipline may be rightly considered an operation of the church parallel in meaning to (adult) baptism.[97] And as to another aspect we are reminded of Conrad Grebel's statement in his letter to Thomas Müntzer (September 1524), where he said that the Lord's Supper "should not be practiced without *previous* attention to the rule of Christ (Matthew 18). For without that rule people would just run after externals. The inner matter, that is, brotherly love, is passed by if both brethren and false brethren eat the Supper together."[98]

The application of church discipline including the ban is possible, however, under only one condition, not lightly attained: charismatic authority, which gives power to either the assembled church — the brotherhood, as a corporate body; or to its appointed leaders — the overseers ("bishops") and elders. Wherever such genuine authority is lacking the "power of the keys" is lost too, or misused; and discipline becomes burdensome if not arbitrary, unless neglected altogether. But there is still another necessary condition, not easily attained if this discipline is to assume the true function of a "healing plaster" within the church, as Hubmaier once called it.[99] Any form of discipline within the true church must be conceived as an instrument of brotherly, redeeming love. The borderline between brotherly admonition on the one hand and outright condemnation of the failing brother on the other hand is narrow indeed, and the temptation to some forms of self-righteousness or even the carnal exertion of power is always close at hand. One need only think of the Puritans and their handling of church discipline to realize this inherent danger. Many cases among the Dutch Doopsgezinden of the sixteenth century, and among the Amish of later times,[100] show the ever-present ambivalence in the idea of church discipline. The numerous splits and divisions (as for instance the great conflict of 1533 in Moravia when Hutterites, Philippites, and Gabrielites separated in anything but a loving spirit) are illustrations enough of the difficulty of attaining the high ideal of "the rule of Christ."

And yet, "where there is no brotherly admonition, no church is to be found," said Hubmaier succinctly.[101] The rule of Christ implies a clearly indicated procedure: first a private rebuke, then corporate admonition by the church, and eventually disciplinary action: either the minor or major ban with exclusion; and (mainly in the Netherlands) also avoidance.[102] But the rule of Christ implies also — and foremost — forgiveness whenever the failing brother repents.[103] Readmission is certainly an essential part of the church's supreme authority and an indication of its inner health.

Two basic tracts by Balthasar Hubmaier gave direction and clarification to the rising Anabaptist movement: *Von der brüderlichen Strafe* and *Von dem christlichen Bann*, both written in late 1526 and printed at Nicolsburg in 1527, immediately preceding the larger tract *Von der Freiheit des Willens* (1527).[104] The two subjects actually belong together: the recognition of man's freedom of decision on the one hand, and the necessity of disciplining this will by means of the ban on the other hand. In the tract on *Brotherly Admonition* (or *Punishment*) emphasis is laid on the loving intent in all this disciplining.[105] Its justification, however, is seen in the baptismal pledge (*Taufgelübde*) of all those who constitute the true church. In other words, church and discipline belong together. The next tract on the ban discusses at length also the subject of shunning (*Meidung*) of the excommunicated member. Banning must never be done out of a feeling of hatred or related passions, for the baptismal pledge always implies the obligation to love even the excommunicated one, whom one should receive back into the church whenever he is ready to say "mea culpa." The parable of the Prodigal Son furnishes a fine example for this idea of total forgiveness.[106]

Contemporary with Hubmaier's books are the still more influential *Seven Articles of Schleitheim* (February 1527). Here Article Two deals expressly with the ban,[107] advising that any such act of disciplining ought to be done prior to the breaking of the bread, "that we may break and eat one loaf with one mind and in one love, and may drink of one cup."[108] The power of discipline must be looked at as beneficial in helping the failing brother to come back upon the right path which he had in one way or another abandoned. (Nothing is said about shunning or avoidance.)

At the important disputation at Zofingen, Switzerland, in July 1532, the brethren explained to their opponents, the Zwinglian clergy, how they handled the ban and exclusion. "No one shall be banned," they declared, "unless he has committed an open sin." "Open sin" they defined in terms of those abominations mentioned in Galatians 5, which exclude from the kingdom of God.[109] The issue of avoidance was not touched upon, since it was not yet an issue.

Also Peter Riedemann deals with exclusion and readmission in his *Rechenschaft* of 1541, but strangely enough he does so only at the end of his book and then in summary fashion. He makes a fine distinction between those who "sin willfully" and are to be punished accordingly, and those who sin "in haste," through the weakness of the flesh. They too deserve some punishment but should not be separated completely and excluded from all fellowship as the former.[110] It is a distinction somewhat reminiscent of a reference by Hans Hut in his *Christlicher Unterricht* to failing brethren of the second type: "And even though such a man sins and fails, yet not out of sheer pleasure (*geschieht nicht mit Lust*) for this reason he will not be condemned altogether. . . ."[111] Judging by the records of the *Great Chronicle* the cases of disciplining among the Hutterites are rather rare, and apply in most cases to differences of a doctrinal nature between the church and some fringe characters in the group.[112]

Of course, the door to readmission into the fellowship was always open for those who showed genuine repentance and were willing to submit to the authority of the church and its leaders. Then as now the "deviant" is the great exception.[113] It is the proof of the inner strength of this brotherhood-church and its spiritual foundations which in the formative first two generations had without doubt a truly existential character.

(2) *The Teaching Office of the Church*

The teaching office was a point of prime concern among the brethren from the very beginning. In the oldest-known church discipline, that of Bern, Switzerland, of 1526/27, the first article begins by saying that the brethren should assemble several times a week if possible in order to be instructed in their faith and also to exhort each other to remain steadfast in that faith. Likewise the first article of the Schleitheim articles of 1527 says of the office of the shepherd (*Hirt*) that it is his duty to read the Scriptures to the brethren, to expound them, to exhort and to teach, to lead out in observing the Lord's Supper, and to be concerned with the discipline of the group. And finally among the Hutterites the preacher has always been called *Lehrer* (teacher) because teaching the Holy Scriptures and expounding them is his foremost and most responsible task.

Sources on the conduct of worship among Anabaptists during the sixteenth century are almost nonexistent.[114] Only Peter Riedemann in his chapter "Concerning Coming Together" briefly describes what was done at such occasions. "First they prayed and gave thanks to God. Then they proceeded to proclaim the Lord's Word faithfully, encouraging the heart of the listeners to fear the Lord and to remain in his fear." Outside Moravia, however, regularly organized activity of this nature was most difficult. And there can be no doubt that teaching — that is, instructing and strengthening the brethren in their faith — was the main program wherever brethren managed to assemble.

Very little is known about the preparation of the youth for the decisive step of adult baptism. In the early days, for instance, during the "apostolate" of Hans Hut, conversion was spontaneous; the apostle simply testified to his own faith and thereby won hundreds and hundreds to his way. It was rather different once churches had been established in which youth could grow up in the atmosphere of this "church under the cross." Would they, too, go through an experience of authentic regeneration? Or would they tend to accept baptism on faith more out of the desire to preserve the new tradition and by this to perpetuate the "kingdom-nucleus" even beyond the first two or three generations?

In their "Golden Period" (c. 1560-90) the Hutterites drew up their special form of catechetical instruction, the *Taufreden*,[115] probably during the time of Peter Walpot (d. 1578). These standardized *Taufreden* are still used, traditionally preceding the Sunday of baptism, though this practice has become a far cry from the spiritual dynamic of the generation of the founding fathers. Next to nothing is known outside the Hutterite fold concerning such practices even though we may assume the existence of some such forms of instructional activities in Swiss and Dutch Anabaptism also.

Originally the leaders were simply there, thanks to their self-understanding of a special calling to such leadership. Besides presiding at the ordinances, their task was predominantly that of teaching and interpreting Holy Writ. Soon, however, the need was felt for a proliferation of this office, whereupon they allowed the lot to decide among those who were deemed worthy of being considered by the *Gemeinde*. Among the Hutterites in particular, a serious problem arose whether there should be full equality among the brethren including the teacher, or whether the *Diener des Wortes* (preacher) should receive "double honor" according to the apostolic injunction in 1 Timothy 5:17. The brotherhood then asked Peter Riedemann, at that time imprisoned, to give his opinion; he counseled them to keep the apostolic pattern unchanged. It was accepted and has remained this way to the present.[116] The *Diener des Wortes* was accepted as the instructor in the interpretation of Holy Scriptures and was also given more time and better quarters to devote himself to such a responsible task. Beginning with the 1560s, the Diener also began to write commentaries, expositions of the books of the Bible, which have remained to this day the very foundation of Christian learning among the Hutterites. It is a compelling feature of Anabaptist history that the brethren were so amazingly well informed about the Bible that no outsider could ever convince them to accept the different understanding of the theologians of the established churches. At trials one is constantly amazed at their familiarity with the entire Scripture, including some Apocryphal books, and at the skill of their interpretation — proof of their intense and all-engrossing occupation with the Bible, both at home alone, and in group Bible study with their fellow believers. As a rule their arguments sound convincing indeed, and deeply impressed judges and authorities at most Anabaptist trials.

Since the Anabaptists as a rule shut themselves off from the outside world, not caring for the cultural activities of their times, the Bible became their exclusive intellectual habitat. In it they lived, and with it they died. This aspect still holds true with regard to the present-day Hutterites, as well as the Amish, who continue to bypass contemporary civilization and go on living like their forefathers in the world of the Bible.

(3) *Outreach and Mission of the Church*[117]

The third agency for the maintenance of a living church body is mission. It might be considered almost axiomatic that as long as a church is spiritually alive it wants to grow, and mission is at least one avenue to this end. In this field the Anabaptists achieved something unique for their time. The great Protestant church bodies, the territorial mass churches of the sixteenth century, were not really interested in this type of work — since everybody belonged to the "established" church by virtue of infant baptism. Little effort was therefore expended to win the masses, not even spiritually, by what today would properly be called "evangelism." Faith comes through hearing, the Apostle Paul taught; hence regular attendance at the Sunday sermons was all that was required. Beyond that the masses remained unaffected until well into the seventeenth century when Pietism changed the spiritual climate. Neither the Catholic clergy nor Protestant orthodoxy gave much thought to the inner conversion of the population.

It was different with the Anabaptists, whose very existence was based on this very principle of inner renewal and personal commitment. To them the Great Commission (Matthew 28) was the guiding principle of all activities toward outreach. Their motivations were of course manifold. A person who himself had passed through the tremendous experience of rebirth was naturally motivated to go out and proclaim his new insights and hopes to everyone willing to listen. To this was added, particularly in the earlier period up to about 1540, a strong apocalyptic zeal. The brethren lived, as was discussed earlier in this study, in the atmosphere of tense expectation of the imminent inbreak of the kingdom of God. They were therefore certain that one who was unwilling to turn away from the evil life of the "world" would have to face a bitter judgment on the last day. Thus the brethren felt it their responsibility to spread their message to as many as could be reached, unmindful of the price they might be asked to pay. The famous Martyrs' Synod at Augsburg in August 1527 might serve as a good illustration — a modern author has correctly called it an "Anabaptist mission conference."[118] Within a few months many of the over sixty participants had been arrested and put to death. But dangers of that kind did not lessen the "apostolic" zeal of these early brethren, who felt so akin to the frame of mind of the Apostles of the primitive church.[119]

But even after the eschatological expectations had faded out, Anabaptist mission work continued unabated and with it their apostolic kerygma: "Repent and be baptized for the remission of your sins" (Acts 2:38). To this was added the urgent invitation to join the "true" church of Christ newly reestablished. Anabaptist mission was, to be sure, a form of "proselytizing," inasmuch as their audience already belonged to some church, Catholic or Lutheran. In fact, Hutterites were eager to work even among other Anabaptists, such as the "Swiss Brethren."[120]

It is understandable that such absolutistic claims led to an urge to spread the message, or better, to "collect" every genuine believer and to bring him into the fold of the newly established Anabaptist congregations. That the Hutterites in particular with their well-established Bruderhofs in Moravia were especially successful may easily be seen. A steady stream of converts moved to this "promised land" of Moravia, even long after the eschatological enthusiasm had ceased as a motivation.[121] The theology of the kingdom remained, as the spiritual rationale of such endeavors — in marked contrast with the pietistic mission work of later times which centered almost exclusively around the idea of the salvation of the individual person, with but little attention to the brotherhood concept.

Details about all these Anabaptist activities and their theological background are far better known from Hutterite sources than from those of any other group, where records are less plentiful. Thus, for instance, we know fairly well the solemnity with which their missioners (*Sendboten*) were sent out on their dangerous assignments in early spring of each year.[122] On this occasion the brethren would sing a hymn of great emotional depth which strengthened both those who were about to leave and those who remained at home.[123] Of course everyone who had committed himself to a life of discipleship was therefore also a potential missioner, since the traditional distinction between clergy and laity had little place in these brotherhoods. Here the principle of "priesthood of all believers" had become full reality and was accepted without reservation. All members were God's chosen servants and messengers who felt it to be their very call to propagate their faith in the same way as the apostles had done in the primitive church: They "went every where preaching the word" (Acts 8:4).

George Williams in his *Radical Reformation* says:

A new kind of Christian had emerged in the course of the Radical Reformation, a composite of the medieval pilgrim to Jerusalem, the ancient martyr of the heavenly Jerusalem, and the emissary of the neo-apostolic Jerusalem. This new kind of Christian was not a reformer but a *converter*, not a parishioner but a sojourner in this world whose true citizenship was in heaven.[124]

These words, with which Williams closes the chapter on "Sectarian Ecumenicity," are so much to the point that we, too, use them to conclude this last section of our analysis of Anabaptist ecclesiology.

———

Three activities have been considered in this section: the ban, teaching, and outreach. The basic task was to perpetuate the church as it was conceived and also to maintain its inner purity. All three activities were practiced with utmost dedication and a sense of personal responsibility, as was befitting a program of such loftiness. Yet we know that this high vision did not prevail in its unadulterated form for more than three generations at the most. Why, one may ask, did the *existential quality* of the Anabaptist church fade away even where persecution did not destroy its external situation? This is a question of profound historical significance. In a study which centers on "theology" there is no way of answering it satisfactorily. For it is essentially a question of a historic or sociological nature. One could, of course, point to John 3:8: "The wind bloweth where it listeth." But that would hardly be an adequate answer. In the final analysis the kingdom of God is not a work of men even where the most selfless dedication prevails. It is an event promised for the end of time. One may hope and prepare for it. But the rest reaches beyond human understanding.

Footnotes to "Ecclesiology"

1. Franklin H. Littell, *The Anabaptist View of the Church* (Second edition, Boston, 1958).

2. See "Restitution," *ME*, IV, 303, 304 where the arguments pro and con are discussed.

3. Cornelius Krahn, "Menno Simons' Concept of the Church," in *A Legacy of Faith*, ed., Cornelius J. Dyck (Newton, Kansas, 1962), p. 23.

4. Harold S. Bender, "The Anabaptist Theology of Discipleship," *MQR*, XXIII (1950), 26; see also Bender's profound article, "Church," *ME*, I, 594-597.

5. First published in 1560, later a part of the *Enchiridion* of 1564. See the fine English translation in George H. Williams' *Spiritual and Anabaptist Writers* (1957), 228-260, with good introduction and notes.

6. In John H. Yoder's book, *Täufertum und Reformation in der Schweiz, I. Die Gespräche zwischen Täufern und Reformatoren, 1523-1538* (1962), one learns that all the elaborate debates between representatives of the official church and the Anabaptists centered almost exclusively around the question: "What kind of church shall we establish?" All other doctrinal questions dropped into the background.

7. Dirck Philips, in his *Van die Ghemeynte Godts* (1560), says expressly: "The congregation of the Lord is the Holy City, the New Jerusalem, coming down from God out of heaven" (Revelation 21:2), Williams, *op. cit.*, 255.

8. Franklin H. Littell, *op. cit.*, 44.

9. Ernst Troeltsch, *The Social Teaching of the Christian Churches* (German ed., 1911; Eng. ed. 1931; paperback 1960). Chapter 1: "Influence of Stoicism on the Doctrine of the State," where the important distinction between "absolute and relative natural law" is introduced.

10. Erland Waltner, "The Anabaptist Conception of the Church," *MQR*, XXV (1951), 5-16.

11. Peter Rideman, *Account of Our Religion* (1950), 39, 40, and 41. This *Rechenschaft* was written while Riedemann was in prison in Hesse for two and a half years. See *ME*, IV.

12. *Ibid.*, 42, 43.

13. Pilgram Marpeck, *Verantwortung*, 294.

14. Franz Heimann, "The Hutterite Doctrine of the Church and Common Life," *MQR*, XXVI (1952), 156.

15. Littell calls this aspect "the eschatological atmosphere," *op. cit.*, 37, 44.

16. The Bainton school in church history, also Littell, Frank Wray, and Walther Köhler. See my article "Restitution," *ME*, IV.

17. Littell, *op. cit.*, chapters II and III.

18. Heimann, *op. cit.*, 142, 156.

19. Also Beatrice Jenny, *Das Schleitheim Täuferbekenntnis*, 1527 (Schaffhausen, 1951), 51, speaks of "empirische Abendmahlsgemeinde," without, however, following through with this idea.

20. Heimann, *op. cit.*, 46.

21. *Ibid.*, 156.

22. Christian Meyer, "Die Wiedertäufer in Augsburg," in *Zeitschrift des Historischen Vereins für Schwaben und Neuburg*, I. (1874), 230, 243, 244.

23. K. Schornbaum, ed., *Quellen zur Geschichte der Täufer*, II, *Markgraftum Brandenburg (Bayern I)* (1934), 49, 50.

24. Herbert Klassen, "Ambrosius Spittelmeyer," *MQR*, XXXII (1958), 270.

25. J. C. Wenger, "Covenant Theology," *ME*, I, 726, 727.

26. John J. Kiwiet, *Pilgram Marbeck, sein Kreis und seine Theologie* (Kassel, 1957), devotes the entire chapter ten to the idea of *Bundesgemeinde*. He notes that in Littell's study (above, note 1) this idea of covenant surprisingly is not mentioned at all.

The *Vermanung* was first written by Bernt Rothmann in the Low German, *Confession of the Two Sacraments* (1534), then translated into the South German tongue and revised by Marpeck.

27. Klassen, *op. cit.*, 265.

28. *Ibid.*, 270.

29. Balthasar Hubmaier, *Schriften*, ed., T. Bergsten (1962), 178.

30. Müller, *Glaubenszeugnisse oberdeutscher Taufgesinnter* (Leipzig, 1938), 36.

31. *Ibid.*, 60, 67.

32. *Ibid.*, 109.

33. *Ibid.*, 138.

34. *Ibid.*, 222, 223.

35. The word "motive" is not a theological term but it may help in the present context. The three motives are discussed by Friedmann, "The Christian Communism of the Hutterite Brethren," *ARG* (1955), 204-207. Also in my *Hutterite Studies* (1961), 82-85.

36. Friedmann, "An Epistle Concerning Communal Life; a Hutterite Manifesto of 1650," *MQR*, XXXIV (1960), 252. Also Andreas Ehrenpreis, *Sendbrief* (1930), 19.

37. See Bender's very helpful article "Perfectionism," *ME*, IV, 1114-1115. Though brief it deserves close attention.

38. See the elaborate article "Ban" by Christian Neff, *ME*, I, 219-223.

39. I am here following a suggestion by Elsa Bernhofer, *Täuferische Denkweise und Lebensform im Spiegel ober- und mitteldeutscher Täuferverhöre* (PhD dissertation, Freiburg i.B., Germany, 1955) [a ms copy in the Mennonite Historical Library, Goshen College]. The following scheme, however, is mine. The Bernhofer dissertation is one of the best in the field.

40. A hidden offense, a sinning in thought only, is of course not socially controllable and therefore not subject to church discipline. Georg Blaurock said in 1526: "If someone cherishes sin in his heart clandestinely, we would not call such a one to account. Only open sins and offenses have to be judged by the church." Von Muralt and W. Schmidt, *Quellen zur Geschichte der Täufer in der Schweiz*, I (Zurich, 1952), 215-217.

41. The ordinance of "ban and forgiveness" will be treated in greater detail in the second part of this chapter on "Ecclesiology." We omit therefore any further discussion at this place where only those elements are at issue which constitute the church idea of the Anabaptists.

42. Bender's article "Church," *ME*, I, 595, first column.

43. I owe this reference to the rather challenging study by Jean Séguy in the French Mennonite monthly magazine *Christ Seul*, "Les trois plus anciennes disciplines de l'Anabaptisme," January-February 1967; text in Ernst Müller, *Geschichte der Bernischen Täufer* (1895), 37, 38.

44. It is found as an insert in the Great Chronicle of the Hutterites, yet erroneously placed in the year 1529. Rudolf Wolkan, ed., *Geschichtsbuch der Hutterischen Brüder* (1923), 60, 61, or A. J. F. Zieglschmid, ed., *Die älteste Chronik* (1943), 83-85. Text and discussion in Friedmann, "The Oldest Church Discipline of the Anabaptists," *MQR*, XXIX (1955), 162-166; plus corrections, *ibid.*, 1956, 236-237.

45. See "Rattenberg" by Friedmann, *ME*, IV.

46. See Beatrice Jenny, *op. cit.*, where the text is also reproduced. English text of the *Vereinigung*, *MQR*, XIX (1945), 243-253, and various reprints.

47. See Friedmann, "Rechenschaft unserer Religion, Lehre und Glaubens," *ME*, IV, 259-261. This is the only comprehensive treatment of the book. Franz Heimann's excellent study (above, note 14) selected only a few special topics.

48. In its English edition, 1950, it comprises 225 pages.

49. Published by Heinold Fast in *Der linke Flügel der Reformation* (Bremen, 1962), 130-137. English translation by William Klassen, *MQR*, XXXVIII (1964), 354-356. See

also Gerhard Hein's article "Scharnschlager," *ME*, IV.

50. Heinold Fast, "Pilgram Marpeck und das oberdeutsche Täufertum, ein neuer Handschriftenfund," *ARG* (1956), 212-242.

51. Ethelbert Stauffer, "Die Märtyrertheologie der Täufer," *Zeitschrift für Kirchengeschichte* (1933), English translation, *MQR*, XIX (1945), 179-214.

52. Williams, *Spiritualist and Anabaptist Writers* (1957), 80, 84.

53. Yoder, *Täufertum und Reformation im Gespräch* (Zürich, 1968), 194.

54. See *ML*, II, article "Lochy," for pictures.

55. Harold S. Bender, "The Anabaptists and Religious Liberty," *MQR*, XXIX (1955), 99. Reprinted as a Facet Book by Fortress Press, 1970 (p. 11).

56. *Ibid.*

57. *Ibid.*, 91.

58. *Die älteste Chronik*, ed., Zieglschmid (1943), 44: "So ist der Glaube nicht zu nöten [zwingen] sondern ein Gab Gottes." For another good example of this spirit see the Confession of Faith by the imprisoned brother Claus Felbinger, 1560, *MQR*, XXIX (1955), 149.

59. The only full-length treatment on the baptismal theology of the Anabaptists is the prize-winning book by Rollin S. Armour, *Anabaptist Baptism: A Representative Study* (Scottdale, Pa., 1966). This is an excellent study with a very adequate grasp of the genius of Anabaptism.

60. Pilgram Marpeck, *Verantwortung* (Wien, 1929), 85 (in the XVII, *Red*). Here Marpeck refers to the Greek term "eperotema" as meaning "interrogacio, das heisst das Zusagen, durch Fragen [offenbar Bezeugnis] oder auch Verteidigung eines guten Gewissens."

61. Pilgram Marpeck, *Vermahnung (Gedenkschrift zum 400-jährigen Jubiläum der Mennoniten oder Taufgesinnten*, 1925), 126, 127, 202, 209. The RSV [English] Bible has "appeal" from which term no theological doctrine could be deduced. Philologically "pledge" would perhaps be the most fitting translation.

62. Luther has "Bad der Wiedergeburt," while the King James version has "washing" of regeneration.

63. *Vermahnung*, 209.

64. "Consent" does not fully render the idea of *Verwilligung*. "Surrender" is perhaps more adequate, since the brethren were thinking of surrender of self-will to the will of God.

65. *Glaubenszeugnisse*, 20.

66. See also *Täuferakten, Bayern I*, 112 and *passim*.

67. Paul Wappler, *Täuferbewegung in Thüringen* (1913), 329; also John Oyer, "Anabaptism in Central Germany," *MQR*, XXXV (1961), 8, 9.

68. *Vermahnung*, 209.

69. *Ibid.*, 208.

70. Hubmaier, *Schriften*, 136.

71. *Ibid.*, 137.

72. *Glaubenszeugnisse*, 23, 24.

73. Leonhard Schiemer, *Von dreyerley Tauff*, in *Glaubenszeugnisse*, 78, 79, where "baptism with blood" is discussed at some length. We may justly ask where this idea might have originated. Since neither Denck nor Hubmaier taught it, it seems fair to ascribe its origin to Hans Hut from whom Schiemer must have learned of it. The ubiquitous persecution, of course, was reason enough for such a doctrine.

74. "Die rechte Taufe ist nichts anderes denn ein Streit mit der Sünde durch das ganze Leben" (*Glaubenszeugnisse*, 25).

75. Thomas Müntzer, *Protestation und Entbietung* (1524), in O. H. Brandt, *Thomas Müntzer, sein Leben und seine Schriften* (Jena, 1933), 142.

76. *Glaubenszeugnisse*, 25.

77. *Ibid.*, 79.

78. *Ibid.*, 78.

79. *Ibid.*, 78, 79.

80. Hans Schlaffer said succinctly: "Whosoever suffers in the flesh stops sinning." At that time (1527) he was in jail in Schwaz, Tirol (*Glaubenszeugnisse*, 89). This is, of course, a paraphrase of 1 Peter 4:1. "Whosoever has suffered in the flesh has ceased from sin."

81. See my article, "Lord's Supper," *ME*, III, 394.

82. Friedmann, *Glaubenszeugnisse oberdeutscher Taufgesinnter*, II, 1967 (full text).

83. John Oyer, "Anabaptism in Central Germany," *MQR*, XXXV (1961), 24.

84. Rudolf, Otto, *The Kingdom of God and the Son of Man* (German ed. 1930; second English edition 1943).

85. *Ibid.*, 311.

86. *Ibid.*, 261.

87. *Ibid.*, 312.

88. *Ibid.*

89. Luther mentioned this parable in his sermon: "Von dem hochwürdigen Sakrament des heiligen wahren Leichnams Christi" 1519 (Weimarer Ausgabe). See Lydia Müller, *Der Kommunismus der mährischen Wiedertäufer* (Leipzig, 1927), 66.

90. *Täuferakten Bayern I* (note 23), 141. Also Wiswedel, *Bilder und Führergestalten*, II (1930), 43, 44.

91. *Vermahnung*, 257.

92. Could it have been Eusebius' renowned *Church History*, so popular among Anabaptists?

93. Cornelius Krahn, *Menno Simons* (Karlsruhe, 1936), 142, note 177; taken from Menno Simons, *Opera Omnia*, 1646, fol. 26a. Here translated from the Dutch.

94. Friedmann, "Claus Felbinger's Confession of Faith of 1560," *MQR*, XXIX (1955), 153, also note 9.

95. See "A Notable Hutterite Document," ed., Friedmann, *MQR*, XXXI (1957), 22 ff. The "Item 94" is on pp. 45, 46.

96. See Friedmann, "An Epistle Concerning Communal Life, a Hutterite Manifesto of 1650 and Its Modern Paraphrase," *MQR*, XXXIV (1960), 259, in the section "The Meal of Community."

97. See article "Ban" by Christian Neff in *ME*, I, 219-223.

98. Williams, *Spiritual and Anabaptist Writers* (1957), 77.

99. "Von der brüderlichen Strafe," in Balthasar Hubmaier, *Schriften*, 343, marginal gloss, reading: "Die brüderliche Straff ist ein hailsam pflaster."

100. For details see "Ban," *ME*, I.

101. Hubmaier, *Schriften*, 339. I am not sure whether "admonition" is here the proper rendering for "straff," which can also mean "punishment" or "discipline."

102. See article "Avoidance" in *ME*, I, 200, 201, and "Marital Avoidance" in *ME*, III, 486, 487. The great majority of Swiss and South German Anabaptists never practiced this principle. Only the Amish insisted on it from the time of the division of 1693.

103. John H. Yoder called my attention to the fact that what the King James Version translated as "binding and loosing," the *New English Bible* rendered with "forbid and allow." See the informative pamphlet No. 14 of the pamphlet series *Concern* (Scottdale, Pa.), 1967, dealing with forgiveness.

104. Hubmaier, *Schriften*, 367-378.

105. *Ibid.*, 343, 346.

106. There we find even the advice that one has to be of help if the excommunicated brother is in need. The *Liebespflicht* (obligation to love) always has precedence over the rule of discipline. Unfortunately, this principle was not always obeyed during the long history of Anabaptism.

107. English translation, *MQR*, XIX (1945), 248. Michael Sattler meant excommuni-

cation, not shunning, as it was practiced by the Obbenites in the Netherlands and is still practiced today by the Amish.

108. Beatrice Jenny (*Das Schleitheimer Täuferbekenntnis*) discusses at great length the issue of church discipline, quoting also Michael Sattler's great Epistle to the Church in Horb, 1527, which contains a stark warning: "Be on your guard lest you, too, learn such evil." But then he closes: "But practice such banning according to Christ's commandment with all your love and with compassion for their cold hearts."

109. Quoted according to *ME*, I, 221.

110. English edition, 1950, 131, 132.

111. *Glaubenszeugnisse*, 36.

112. For instance we learn of the rather annoying case in 1576 of a certain Otto Niederländer who argued among his brethren about original sin. The case is very involved; at the end the man was excluded from the brotherhood lest he start unrest among the brethren who became confused as to the correctness of the teachings of their elders. See *Geschichtsbuch* (1923), 369.

113. Today, less than one percent of the adult population, according to John A. Hostetler.

114. Cf. Friedmann, "Hutterite Worship and Preaching," *MQR*, XL (1966), 5-26. This is, as far as is known, the only study on Anabaptist liturgy and worship.

115. See "Taufreden" by Friedmann in *ME*, IV, 686.

116. See "Ministers, Hutterite, Special Honors," by Friedmann, *ME*, III; 698, 699, also J. Loserth, *Der Communismus der Wiedertäufer in Mähren* (Wien, 1894), 95, note 2.

117. Concerning Anabaptist mission see Wiswedel's great study in *ARG*, 1943 and 1948; also Littell, "The Anabaptist Theology of Mission," *MQR*, XXI (1947), 5-17, and the chapter "The Great Commission," in Littell's *The Anabaptist View of the Church* (1958), Chapter V. Finally the great study by Wolfgang Schäufele, *Das missionarische Bewusstsein und Wirken der Täufer* (Neukirchner Verlag, 1966), 356 pages, with exhaustive bibliography. By far the most thorough study of this issue, using also unpublished sources.

118. Schäufele, *op. cit.*, "Die Augsburger Missionskonferenz," 148-152.

119. Therefore forbidding any comparison with modern missionaries and evangelists, who represent a completely different genius.

120. The Anabaptists had little success among the non-German-speaking peoples, such as, for instance, the Slavs in Moravia or Bohemia, the Hungarians and Rumanians, not to speak of French-language areas.

121. Cf. J. G. Neumann, "Nach und von Mähren. Aus der Täufergeschichte des 16. und 17. Jahrhunderts," *ARG*, 1957, 75-90. Some people estimated the number of Hutterites at their peak period (c. 1570-90) as high as 30,000 souls, children included.

122. W. Schäufele, *op. cit.*, 171, 172 ("Aussendungsfeierlichkeiten"), also Johann Loserth, *Der Communismus der Wiedertäufer in Mähren*, p. 94 of the reprint (or p. 228 of the article in *Archiv für österreichische Geschichte*, V. 81). The sources for mission among the Hutterites are named in Friedmann, *Die Schriften der Hutterischen Täufergemeinschaften*, 1965 (Denkschriften der österreichischen Akademie der Wissenchaften, Vol. 86), 163-64.

123. "O Gott, so thue uns sterckhen / Das wir es mögen thuen / Alzeit treulich aufmerckhen / Zu suechen dein eer und ruem." Stanza 7 of a hymn of 23 stanzas, composed by a Hutterite brother in 1568. Cf. R. Wolkan, *Lieder der Wiedertäufer*, Berlin, 1903, 206-209. Wolkan calls it one of the most moving hymns ever composed by Anabaptists. Reproduced also in *Lieder der Hutterischen Brüder* (1914), 650-652.

124. Williams, *The Radical Reformation*, p. 844. Here the *Sendboten* (missioners) are called "prophets."

CONCLUSION

To say that a "theology of Anabaptism" does not even exist is certainly a misleading statement. Yet, we started our essay with the thesis that there are pertinent arguments why a "systematic" theology could not possibly develop in this milieu. The basic vision of the regenerated disciples of Christ was *Nachfolge*, the living by and witnessing to the Spirit, a situation which resisted systematic formulation in categorical terms. Anabaptism, thus runs our thesis, is "existential Christianity," or as we could also call it: concrete, actualized Christianity, reminiscent of the primitive church of the apostles. It is clear that people of this frame of mind were not content to develop a neatly constructed system which would not basically change the "world" and its values. Existential orientation excludes the tendency to systematize. In other words, where witnessing is at stake theorizing stops.

Nevertheless, theology is definitely needed, also in such a venture: that is, a set of ideas concerning God, God's relationship to man, and man's relationship to God and to his fellowmen. Certainly the Gospels contain theology, even though Jesus spoke mainly in parables. This type of theology we called "implicit," that is, it is silently presupposed — in contrast with systematic theology which requires learned men to formulate and expound it.

The traditional Pauline-Augustine theology (versus Johannine or Petrine thought) was revived by Luther and by the Swiss Reformers, Zwingli and Calvin. In its center stands

the concern for the salvation of the individual sinner. Certain sections of the Pauline epistles were selected to develop
the Protestant "sola fide" theology. which teaches in brief
that not by good works but by faith "alone" may the sinner
be saved — whereby the idea of faith remains somewhat undefined. The moral element was toned down by Luther lest
the notion of "merit by works" could creep in again. Basically, the world became secularized and the theology concen-
trated on the individual and his predicament *qua* sinner.

Nothing of this kind belongs to the Anabaptist vision. It
is therefore not allowable to interpret Anabaptism as a sort
of radicalized Protestantism or even as "Protestantism plus
more emphasis on ethics." In this context it might be helpful
to quote an outstanding modern theologian and church historian, Walther Köhler, who in his challenging *Dogmengeschichte als Geschichte des christlichen Selbstbewusstseins*, II
(1951), makes a number of enlightening remarks about
Anabaptism:

> While Luther discovered only religion in his Bible, and Eras-
> mus considered the Sermon on the Mount to be the
> purest proclamation of the Gospel, . . . Anabaptism com-
> bined Luther's anti-Catholic fight against the priesthood
> and works-righteousness with the ethical emphasis of
> Erasmus into an idea of life in which the primitive church
> was to be re-established. [1]

And further: "Anabaptists and Spiritualists reached beyond
Paul, back to the Gospel of Jesus," [2] an idea similarly expressed by Bainton. [3] And finally: "With the Anabaptists the
idea of justification is replaced by the idea of discipleship.
Here Christ is an example or model rather than the 'savior,'" [4]
and he quotes Hans Denck with his saying: "Whosoever follows Christ in his unmerited suffering has accepted it from
him. That is righteousness through grace."

Köhler correctly sensed the difference even though he
did not have at his disposal that wealth of source material,
which we have today, to corroborate such a thesis. "Going
back to the gospel" means reviving the old theology of the

kingdom of God, of the imminent inbreak of the heavenly Jerusalem and one's preparedness for it. Such a "kingdom theology" [5] has a rather different orientation from that of Lutheranism (our main point of reference when speaking of Protestantism). Basic for this kingdom theology is a sharp dualism, but not as with Paul, who contraposed "spirit and flesh," but as with Jesus: "kingdom of God" *versus* "kingdom of darkness" or "kingdom of the prince of this world." [6] Hence the Anabaptist repudiation of the "world" and its values, and the establishment of small nuclei — realms of peace and brotherly love which anticipate the coming kingdom in a small yet genuine way, imperfect to be sure.

This is the basic theological presupposition closely intertwined with eschatological expectation, the certainty that great events cannot be too far off. Though no elaborate prophecy was indulged in (except perhaps with Melchior Hofmann), the mood was the same over much of Europe in the 1520s and early 1530s: the kingdom is coming, "Repent, purify yourself, be baptized, and separate yourself from the world and its inherent wickedness." This gave strength and conviction to the budding movement. No "cheap grace" was allowed; the narrow path is a hard one, few were able to walk it. The rest follows from these premises, and there is no need for further analysis.

As a concluding illustration of this frame of mind, I present here a diagram found in an old Hutterite codex of 1566, the oldest known codex of its kind. The author is not named, but as the same diagram is found at the end of a treatise written by Leonhard Schiemer in the Rattenberg prison in 1527, it is fair to ascribe it to this very profound and concerned brother who wanted to give guidance and instruction to his orphaned Rattenberg congregation of which he was *Vorsteher* or "bishop."

Here it is in an English version. [7]

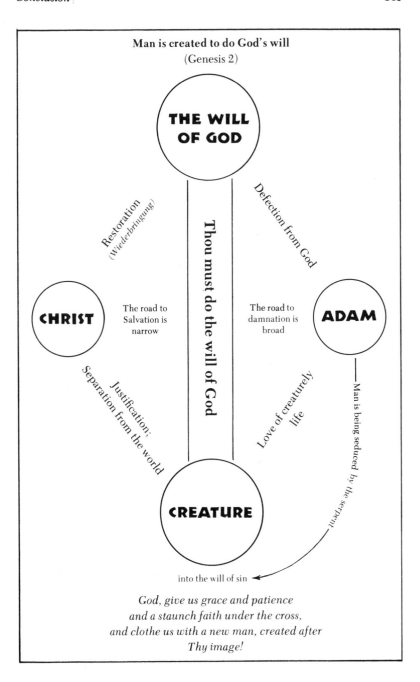

Man is created to do God's will
(Genesis 2)

THE WILL
OF GOD

Restoration
(*Wiederbringung*)

Defection from God

Thou must do the will of God

CHRIST

The road to
Salvation is
narrow

The road to
damnation is
broad

ADAM

Justification;
Separation from the world

Love of creaturely
life

Man is being seduced by the serpent

CREATURE

into the will of sin

*God, give us grace and patience
and a staunch faith under the cross,
and clothe us with a new man, created after
Thy image!*

Footnotes to "Conclusion"

1. Walther Köhler, *Dogmengeschichte als Geschichte des christlichen Selbstbewusstseins* (1951), 85.
2. *Ibid.*, 358.
3. See article "Restitution," *ME*, IV, 304, where Roland H. Bainton is quoted as saying: "The Anabaptists went back further than any other group, and turned exclusively to the New Testament. Even within the New Testament they tended to neglect Paul and to push back to Jesus. That is why [with the Anabaptists] the ideal of "restitution" tends to coincide with the ideal of the imitation of Christ" (letter of 1953).
4. Köhler, *op. cit.*, 356.
5. In recent years this kingdom theology was expounded again by the Blumhardts, father and son, and by Leonhard Ragaz of Zürich (d. 1945).
6. Similar to the ideas of the Essenes. Among the famous Dead Sea Scrolls was found one tract called: "The Warfare Between the Children of Light and the Children of Darkness."
7. First published by Friedmann in *MQR*, XXXIII (1959), 105, and again in his *Hutterite Studies* (1961), 296, in both cases, however, in the original German.

POSTSCRIPT

The essay here presented, a "first" in Anabaptist studies, was originally drafted in the fall of 1964, although it might also be regarded as the result of more than forty years of occupation with the subject matter. Here I want simply to acknowledge my indebtedness to the spiritual climate I experienced through the years within the Associated Mennonite Biblical Seminaries at Goshen and Elkhart, Indiana, and the challenge which the ongoing dialogue produced. In the fall of 1966, I was privileged to deliver five "Menno Simons Lectures" at Bethel College in North Newton, Kansas, where I discussed some salient aspects of this subject, thus further clarifying my position and arguments. I think that the intellectual trend today has ripened enough to make an approach here proposed more readily acceptable and understood.

Kalamazoo, Michigan   R.F.

BIBLIOGRAPHY

Section A
Sources
(predominantly to 1560)

Brüderliche Vereinigung etzlicher Kinder Gottes, etc., 1527, ed. by Walther Köhler in "Flugschriften aus den ersten Jahren der Reformation," 1909. This pamphlet contains the Schleitheim Confession of Faith together with Michael Sattler's letter to the church at Horb, 1527, and the "Acta," the trial and end of Sattler, 1527 (a major source for the Swiss Brethren). See also Jenny in Section B, who likewise edited this document (1951). For an English translation see below under Sattler.

"Confession of the Swiss Brethren in Hesse, 1578," ed. by Theodor Sippell, *Mennonite Quarterly Review* (hereafter *MQR*), XXIII (1949), pp. 24-34; now also in G. Franz, *Täuferakten aus Hessen*, 1951, pp. 404-440. Confession of one H. P. Kuchenbecker.

Ehrenpreis, Andreas (Hutterite bishop), Ein *Sendbrief* an alle diejenigen, so sich rühmen . . . als sonderlich die sich auch Brüder und Schwestern nennen, als Mennisten, Schweizer Brüder und andere mehr . . . *brüderliche Gemeinschaft, das höchste Gebot der Liebe betreffend*. Anno 1652. Aufs Neue herausgegeben von der Hutterischen Brüdern in Amerika, Scottdale, Pa., 1920. (Recent reprints in Canada.)

Fast, Heinold, *Der linke Flügel der Reformation, Glaubenszeugnisse oberdeutscher Täufer, Spiritualisten, Schwärmer und Anti-Trinitarier* (Klassiker des Protestantismus, Vol. IV), Bremen, 1962. Texts in modernized German.

Felbinger, Claus. "Claus Felbinger's Confession of Faith of
1560," ed. by Friedmann, MQR, XXIX (1955), pp.141-161.
Important source.
Fischer, Hans Georg. *Jakob Huter, Leben, Frömmigkeit,
Briefe.* Newton, Kan., 1956. Contains in its Appendix all
eight extant letters by Jacob Huter in modernized German.
Friedmann, Robert. *Glaubenszeugnisse oberdeutscher Taufgesinnter,* Vol. II, 1967. (See below Lydia Müller for Vol. I.)
This volume contains Peter Riedemann's first "Rechen-
schaft" of 1530/1 and the Great Article Book by Peter
Walpot of 1577. Vol. III of *Glaubenszeugnisse,* with the
balance of the sources, is in preparation (no date set).
Franck, Sebastian. *Chronica, Zeytbuch und Geschychtsbibel.*
1531. A most important source. Cf. also article "Chronica,"
etc., in *Mennonite Encyclopedia* [hereafter *ME*], Vol. I,
by Friedmann.
Grebel, Conrad. "Epistle to Thomas Müntzer, September 1524,"
Eng. translation in *Spiritual and Anabaptist Writers,* ed. by
George H. Williams, 1957, pp. 73-85. With most helpful
introduction. Also, *Conrad Grebel's Programmatic Letters
of 1524,* transcribed and translated by J. C. Wenger, Her-
ald Press, 1970.
Handbüchlein wider den Prozess . . . c. 1558. To be published
in Vol. III of *Glaubenszeugnisse,* ed. by Robert Friedmann
and Leonard Gross. Ms. copy in the Mennonite Historical
Library, Goshen College. See also Wiswedel-Friedmann in
Section B.
Hege, Christian. "Pilgram Marbeck's Vermahnung," in
*Gedenkschrift zum 400-jährigen Jubiläum der Mennoniten
oder Taufgesinnten,* Ludwigshafen, 1925, pp. 178-282.
Very important source.
Hillerbrand, Hans Joachim. "Ein Täuferbekenntnis aus dem
16. Jahrhundert" (c. 1540), *Archiv für Reformationsge-
schichte* (hereafter *ARG*), 1959, pp. 40-44.
Hubmaier, Balthasar. *Schriften,* ed. by G. Westin and T. Berg-
sten, 1962. Excellent edition with fine introductions.
Hutter, Jakob. "Last Epistle from Tirol, 1535," MQR, XXXIV
(1960), pp. 37-47.

————. "Epistle Concerning the Schism in Moravia in 1533," *MQR*, XXXVIII (1964), pp. 329-343. Both editions by Friedmann.

Kunstbuch of 1561, to be published in the Täuferakten series by Heinold Fast. Ms. copy in Mennonite Historical Library at Goshen College, Goshen, Ind. A very important source from the Marpeck brotherhood. The oldest extant Anabaptist codex. See below under Heinold Fast in Section B.

Loserth, Johann (ed.). *Pilgram Marbeck's Antwort auf Kaspar Schwenckfelds Beurteilung des Buches der Bundesbezeugung von 1542.* Wien, 1929 (592 pages, octavo). Very important source.

Müller, Lydia. *Glaubenszeugnisse oberdeutscher Taufgesinnter.* Vol. I, 1938. Thus far the best source publication for South German-Austrian Anabaptists, even though some documents are unfortunately abbreviated.

"A Notable Hutterite Document Concerning True Surrender and Christian Community of Goods," translated by Kathleen Hasenberg and introduced by Friedmann, *MQR*, XXXI (1957), pp. 22-62. This is "Article Three" of the Great Article Book of 1577; an important source.

Rideman, Peter. *Account of Our Religion, Doctrine and Faith* (1540-1541). Eng. translation by the Society of Brothers, 1950, 1970, Woodcrest, Rifton, N.Y.: Plough Publishing House.

————. *Rechenschaft unserer Religion, Lehr und Glaubens.* Published by the Hutterite Brethren in America (first 1902, now several reprints). A major source. See also Heimann, Franz, in Section B. The name "Riedemann" is spelled a variety of ways. We shall remain with the usual spelling throughout this work, except when quoting from "Rideman," *Account.* . . , where the name is so spelled.

Sattler, Michael. "Brüderliche Vereinigung" (1527). English translation by J. C. Wenger, "The Schleitheim Confession of Faith," *MQR*, XIX (1945), pp. 243-253. For a discussion of it, see Jenny in Section B.

Täuferakten I, Württemberg, 1930; II, *Bayern I,* 1934; IV, *Baden-Pfalz,* 1951; V, *Bayern II,* 1951; VI, *Elsass I,* 1958; VII, *Elsass II,* 1960; X, *Österreich,* 1964. Outside this series: *Hessen,* 1951 (ed., Franz, G.); *Schweiz,* 1952. More volumes in preparation.

van Braght, Thieleman. *The Martyrs Mirror* (of 1660). Eng. translation, Scottdale, Pa.: Mennonite Publishing House. Many reprints: 1938, 1950, 1951, 1964, 1968.

Wenger, J. C., Ed. and trans. of early Anabaptist tracts:

——————. "The Schleitheim Confession. . . ." See above, Sattler.

——————. "Concerning the Satisfaction of Christ," *MQR,* XX (1946), pp. 243-254.

——————. "Concerning Divorce," *MQR,* XXI (1947), 114-119.

——————. "Two Kinds of Obedience," *MQR,* XXI (1947), pp. 18-22.

——————. "Three Swiss Brethren Tracts," *MQR,* XXI (1947), pp. 275-284.

——————. "Two Early Anabaptist Tracts," *MQR,* XXII (1948), pp. 34-42. Containing "An Anabaptist Sermon" of 1527, and "An Exposition of the Lord's Prayer," also 1527, both most likely by Eitelhans Langenmantel.

——————. "Martin Weninger's Vindication [*Rechenschaft*] of Anabaptism, 1535," *MQR,* XXII (1948), 180-187.

——————. "An Early Anabaptist Tract on Hermeneutics" [by MS; likely Michael Sattler], *MQR,* XLII (1968), pp. 26-44.

Williams, George H. (ed.) *Spiritual and Anabaptist Writers, Documents Illustrative of the Radical Reformation* (Library of Christian Classics, XXV), 1957. Most valuable.

Zieglschmid, A.J.F. (ed.) *Die älteste Chronik der Hutterischen Brüder,* Philadelphia, 1943. (See here in particular: "Die fünf Artikel des grössten Streites zwischen uns und der Welt," pp. 269-316.) This is a new edition of the *Geschichtbuch der Hutterischen Brüder,* ed. by Rudolf Wolkan, Wien, 1923.

Section B
Studies and Essays

(Items of major significance for our subject have an asterisk.°)

Althaus, Paul. *Die letzten Dinge.* 8th ed., 1961. The best work on Christian eschatology.°

Armour, Rollin S. *Anabaptist Baptism, a Representative Study.* Studies in Anabaptist and Mennonite History, No. 11. Scottdale, Pa., 1966. An excellent study, received the Brewer prize of the American Society of Church History.°

Augsburger, Myron. "Conversion in Anabaptist Thought," *MQR,* XXXVI (1962), pp. 243-257.

Bauman, Clarence. *Gewaltlosigkeit im Täufertum, eine Untersuchung zur theologischen Ethik des oberdeutschen Täufertums der Reformationszeit.* Leiden, 1968.

Beachy, Alvin. "The Grace of God as Understood by Five Major Anabaptist Writers," *MQR,* XXXVII (1963), pp. 5-33. Condensation of a PhD dissertation at Harvard Divinity School.

—————. "The Theology and Practice of Anabaptist Worship," *MQR,* XL (1966), pp. 163-178. With an added note by R. Friedmann.

Bender, Harold S. "The Anabaptist Vision," *MQR,* XVIII (1944), pp. 67-88. Basic for our interpretation. Latest reprint, Scottdale, Pa., 1972.°

—————."The Anabaptist Theology of Discipleship," *MQR,* XXIV (1950), pp. 25-32.

—————. *Conrad Grebel, Founder of the Swiss Brethren.* Goshen, Ind. See in particular the chapter, "Things Most Certainly Believed," 1950, 1971, pp. 163-208.°

—————. "Theology, Anabaptist," *ME,* Vol. IV, 1959, pp. 704-708. This is the only treatment of our subject, without, however, centering on any particular theory.

—————. "Pilgram Marpeck, Anabaptist Theologian and Civil Engineer," *MQR,* XXXVIII (1964), pp. 231-265. With complete bibliography to 1962. Bender wrote many more articles and studies, mainly for *ME,* such as "Church,"

"Perfectionism," etc., which cannot be listed individually.

Bergsten, Torsten. *Balthasar Hubmaier, seine Stellung zu Reformation und Täufertum.* Kassel, 1961. Excellent.°

————. *Pilgram Marpeck und seine Auseinandersetzung mit Kaspar Schwenckfeld.* Uppsala, Sweden, 1958.

Bernhofer-Pippert, Elsa. *Täuferische Denkweise und Lebensformen im Spiegel oberdeutscher Täuferverhöre.* Mit einem Vorwort von Ernst Walter Zeeden, Münster, Westfalen (Reformationsgeschichtliche Studien und Texte, Heft 96, 1967). An excellent and helpful study, originally a PhD dissertation at Freiburg i.B. University, 1955.°

Bonhoeffer, Dietrich. *The Cost of Discipleship.* 1949, Original in German, 1937.

Bright, John. *The Kingdom of God, the Biblical Concept and Its Meaning for the Church.* Nashville, Tenn.: Abingdon Press, 1953. A companion volume to the book by Rudolf Otto, quoted below.

Brush, John. "Radical Eschatology of the Continental Reformation." PhD dissertation, Yale University Divinity School, 1942. Ms. at Yale Divinity School Library — mainly on Anabaptism.

Burkholder, Lawrence. "The Anabaptist Vision of Discipleship," in *The Recovery of the Anabaptist Vision,* ed. by G. F. Hershberger, 1957, pp. 135-151. Very good.

Duerksen, Rosella Reimer. "Doctrinal Implications in Sixteenth-Century Anabaptist Hymnody," *MQR,* XXXV (1961), pp. 38-50. Excellent.°

Dyck, Cornelius J. "Sinners and Saints," in *A Legacy of Faith,* ed. by C. J. Dyck, Newton, Kan., 1962, pp. 87-102. Excellent.

Fast, Heinold. *Heinrich Bullinger und die Täufer, ein Beitrag zur Historiographie und Theologie im 16. Jahrhundert* (Schriftenreihe des Mennonitischen Geschichtsvereins, Nr. 7.). Karlsruhe, 1959.

————. "Pilgram Marpeck und das oberdeutsche Täufertum, ein neuer Handschriftenfund," *ARG,* 1956, pp. 212-242. Concerns the "Kunstbuch" of 1561.

————. *Der linke Flügel der Reformation, Glaubenszeug-*

*nisse der Täufer, Spiritualisten, Schwärmer und Anti-
trinitarier.* Bremen, 1962. Very fine introductions; see also Section A.

—————. "Bemerkungen zur Taufanschauung der Täufer,"
ARG, 1966, pp. 131-151. A parallel study to the book by
Rollin S. Armour; see above.

Fischer, Hans Georg. "Lutheranism and the Vindication of the
Anabaptist Way," *MQR,* XXVIII (1954), pp. 27-38. Stimulating.°

—————. *Jakob Huter, Leben, Frömmigkeit, Briefe.* Newton, Kan., 1956. See in particular the sections: "Die reli-
giöse Gedankenwelt" and "Zeuge evangelischer
Frömmigkeit."

Friedmann, Robert. *Mennonite Piety Through the Centuries,
Its Genius and Literature.* Goshen, Ind., 1949. See in particular the two chapters: "Concept of the Spirit" and Conclusion."

—————. "The Encounter of Anabaptists . . . with Anti-
Trinitarianism," *MQR,* XXII (1948), pp. 139-162.

—————. "Anabaptism and Protestantism," *MQR,* XXIV
(1950), pp. 12-24.

—————. "Peter Riedemann on Original Sin. . . ," *MQR,*
XXVI (1952), pp. 210-215.

—————. "Recent Interpretations of Anabaptism," *Church
History,* 1955, pp. 132-157.

—————"A Hutterite Book of Medieval Origin," *MQR,* XXX
(1956), pp. 65-71.

—————. "The Doctrine of the Two Worlds," in *The Recovery of the Anabaptist Vision,* ed. by G. F. Hershberger, 1957, pp. 105-118. Basic for the present study. Also
in: Friedmann, Robert. *Hutterite Studies.* Goshen, Ind.,
1961. Collected essays.

—————. "Hutterite Worship and Preaching," *MQR,* XL
(1966), pp. 5-26.

—————. "The Essence of Anabaptist Faith," *MQR,* XLI
(1967), pp. 5-24.

Garrett, James Leo. "The Nature of the Church According to
the Radical Continental Reformation," *MQR,* XXXII (1958),

pp. 111-127. Mainly typology.

Gritsch, E. W. "The Authority of the Inner Word, a Theological Study of the Major Spiritual Reformers of the Sixteenth Century." PhD dissertation, Yale Divinity School, 1962. Copy at the Library of Yale Divinity School.

——————. "Thomas Müentzer and the Origins of Protestant Spiritualism," *MQR*, XXXVII (1963), pp. 172-194.

Hall, Thor. "Possibilities of Erasmian Influence on Hubmaier and Denck in Their Views on the Freedom of Will," *MQR*, XXXV (1961), pp. 149-170. Very helpful.

Heimann, Franz. "The Hutterite Doctrine of Church and Common Life. A Study of Peter Riedemann's Confession of Faith of 1540," *MQR*, XXVI (1952), pp. 22-47; 142-160. Orginally a PhD dissertation, University of Vienna, Austria, 1927. Valuable analyses. Translation and notes by Friedmann.°

Hillerbrand, Hans Joachim. "Anabaptism and Reformation," *Church History*, 1960, pp. 404-424.

——————. "The Origin of Sixteenth Century Anabaptism: Another Look," *ARG*, 1962, pp. 152-180. Stimulating.

Horsch, John. "Faith of the Swiss Brethren," *MQR*, IV (1930), pp. 241-266; and 1931, pp. 7-27. Rich in source references.

Jenny, Beatrice. "Das Schleitheim Täuferbekenntnis 1527," in *Schaffhauser Beiträge zur vaterländischen Geschichte*, Schaffhausen, Switzerland, 1951, pp. 5-81. Also published separately. Part One contains the text of a Bernese manuscript. Part Two is systematic discussion of the "implied theology." Very stimulatingly presented. Originally a Zurich PhD dissertation.°

Kaufman, Gordon. "Some Theological Emphases of the Early Swiss Anabaptists," *MQR*, XXV (1951), pp. 75-99.

Kiwiet, Jan J. *Pilgram Marbeck, ein Führer der Täuferbewegung im süddeutschen Raum*. Kassel, 1957.

Klaassen, Walter. "The Anabaptist View of Word and Spirit." PhD dissertation, University of Oxford, England, 1960. An exceedingly fine study, rather profound.

——————. "Some Anabaptist Views on the Doctrine of the Holy Spirit," *MQR*, XXXV (1961), pp. 130-139. Condensa-

tion of the above study.
——————. "Spiritualization in the Reformation," *MQR*, XXXVII (1963), pp. 67-77.

Klassen, A.D., Jr. "Did Our Forefathers Have a Theology?" *Mennonite Life*, 1956, pp. 184-190.

Klassen, Herbert. "Ambrosius Spittelmayer, His Life and Teachings," *MQR*, XXXII (1958), pp. 251-269. Important contribution.°

——————. "The Life and Teachings of Hans Hut," *MQR*, XXXIII (1959), pp. 171-205, 267-304. Valuable, especially the second part.°

Klassen, William. *Covenant and Community; The Life, Writings and Hermeneutics of Pilgram Marpeck*. Grand Rapids, Mich., 1968.

Köhler, Walther. "Die Züricher Täufer," in *Gedenkschrift zum 400-jährigen Jubiläum der Mennoniten oder Taufgesinnten*, Ludwigshafen, 1925, pp. 48-64.°

——————. *Dogmengeschichte als Geschichte des christlichen Selbstbewusstseins*, Vol. II: *Zeitalter der Reformation*, Tübingen, 1951. Most helpful, with good Index.°

Krahn, Cornelius. "Menno Simons' Concept of the Church," in *A Legacy of Faith*, ed. by C. J. Dyck, Newton, Kan., 1962. pp. 17-30.

——————. *Menno Simons, ein Beitrag zur Geschichte und Theologie der Taufgesinnten*. Karlsruhe, 1936.

Littell, Franklin H. *The Anabaptist View of the Church*. 2nd ed., Boston, 1958. See in particular Chapter V: "The Great Commission," dealing with Anabaptist mission.°

Loserth, Johann. *Dr. Balthasar Hubmaier*. Wien, 1893. Cf. many more of his studies in Anabaptism. See "Loserth," *ME*, III.

McGiffert, A.C., Sr. *Protestant Thought Before Kant*. Reprint as Torch Book, 1911. Though an early product, it is still valuable for Anabaptism.

Mecenseffy, Grete. "Das Verständnis der Taufe bei den süddeutschen Täufern," in *Antwort: Festschrift für Karl Barth*, 1956, pp. 642-646. Very good.

Mennonite Encyclopedia, Harold S. Bender, ed., four volumes,

1955-1959. Indispensable reference work.

Meyer, Christian. "Die Anfänge der Wiedertaufe in Augsburg," in *Zeitschrift des Historischen Vereins für Schwaben
und Neuburg*, Vol. I., 1874, pp. 205-256. Contains the
complete trial records of Hans Hut, 1527.°

Müller, Lydia. *Der Kommunismus der mährischen Wiedertäufer*.
Leipzig, 1927. A study done under Heinrich Böhmer.

Muralt, L. von. *Glauben und Leben der Schweizer Täufer*.
Zürich, 1938.

————. "Zum Problem Reformation und Täufertum,"
Zwingliana, Vol. VI (1934), pp. 65-85.

Neumann, Gerhard J. "Rechtfertigung und Person Christi als
dogmatische Glaubensfragen bei den Täufern der Reformationszeit," *Zeitschrift für Kirchengeschichte*, 1959, pp.
62-74.

————. "Eschatologische und chiliastische Gedanken in der
Reformationszeit, besonders bei den Täufern," in *Die
Welt als Geschichte*, 1959, pp. 58 ff.

————. "The Anabaptist Position on Baptism and the
Lord's Supper," *MQR*, XXXV (1961), pp. 140-149.

Oosterbaan, J. A. "Grace in Dutch Mennonite Theology," in
A Legacy of Faith, ed. by C. J. Dyck, Newton, Kan.,
1962, pp. 69-85.

Otto, Rudolf. *The Kingdom of God and the Son of Man*. 1st
German ed., 1930. 2nd Eng. ed., 1943. Most valuable for
a comparison of Anabaptism and the apostolic church of
Jerusalem. Many ideas and forms are surprisingly parallel.°

Oyer, John S. *Lutheran Reformers Against Anabaptism*. The
Hague, 1964. Highly stimulating for the dialogue between
Protestantism and Anabaptism. Originally a PhD disser-
tation, University of Chicago.

————. "Anabaptism in Central Germany. II: Faith and
Life," *MQR*, XXXV (1961), pp. 5-37. Deals with Anabaptism in Thuringia, mainly with Melchior Rinck. Very
helpful.°

Sachsse, Carl. *Balthasar Hubmaier als Theologe*. Berlin, 1914.
Basic.°

Schäufele, Wolfgang. *Das missionarische Bewusstsein und*

Wirken der Täufer, dargestellt nach oberdeutschen Quellen. Neukirchener Verlag, 1966. Very good.

Séguy, Jean. "Les trois plus anciennes disciplines de l' Anabaptisme," *Christ Seul,* Nos. 1 & 2, Montbéliard, 1967.

Smucker, Don. "Theological Triumph of the Early Anabaptist-Mennonites. . . ," *MQR,* XIX (1945), pp. 5-26. Not based on original research but stimulating.

—————. "Love," *ME,* Vol. III (1959), pp. 404-405.

Stauffer, Ethelbert. "The Anabaptist Theology of Martyrdom," *MQR,* XIX (1945), pp. 179-214. Basic for our study. This is a translation of Stauffer's study in *Zeitschrift für Kirchengeschichte,* 1933.°

Swartzentruber, A. Orley. "The Piety and Theology of the Anabaptist Martyrs in van Braght's *Martyrs Mirror,*" *MQR,* XXVIII (1954), pp. 5-26; 128-142. An outstanding analysis of the subject, most useful for our purpose.°

Verduin, Leonard. *The Reformers and Their Stepchildren.* Eerdmans, 1964. An essay on medieval dissent, and the exhibition of pre-Reformation anticipations of Anabaptist emphases. Stimulating.

Waltner, Erland. "The Anabaptist Conception of the Church," *MQR,* XXV (1951), pp. 5-16. Very clear.

Wappler, Paul, *Die Täuferbewegung in Thüringen, 1526-1584.* Jena, 1913. Contains 297 pages of source material.

Wenger, J. C. *Doctrines of the Mennonites.* 2nd ed., Scottdale, Pa., 1952. With ample quotations from Anabaptist sources.

—————. "Grace and Discipleship in Anabaptism," *MQR,* XXXV (1961), pp. 50-69.

Williams, George H. *The Radical Reformation.* Philadelphia, 1962. Basic; see particularly the last chapter: "Sectarian Ecumenicity." A book of great significance.°

—————. "Sanctification in the Testimony of Several So-called Schwärmer," *MQR,* XLII (1968), pp. 5-25.

Wiswedel, Wilhelm. *Bilder und Führergestalten aus dem Täufertum.* Vol. I, 1928; Vol. II, 1930; Vol. III, 1953. Very helpful and rich in information, taken to a large extent from the so-called "Beck Nachlass" in Brünn.°

—————. "Die alten Täufergemeinden und ihr missionarisches Wirken," *ARG*, 1943, pp. 183-200; 1948, pp. 115-132. Very good.

————. "Inner and Outer Word: A Study in the Anabaptist Doctrine of Scripture," *MQR*, XXVI (1952), pp. 171-191. The same essay in German, *ARG*, 1955. An abbreviated summary in *ME*, Vol. I, "Bible, Inner and Outer Word," pp. 324-328.°

Wiswedel, Wilhelm, and Friedmann, Robert. "The Anabaptists Answer Melanchthon." Part I: "The Handbüchlein of 1558" (Wiswedel)°; Part II: "Some Further Studies Pertaining to the Handbüchlein of 1558" (Friedmann), *MQR*, XXIX (1955), pp. 212-231. See also article "Handbüchlein" by Friedmann in *ME*, Vol. II, pp. 645-646.

Wolkan, Rudolf. *Die Lieder der Wiedertäufer*. Berlin, 1903. Reprint by B. de Graaf, 1964. Most helpful work also for the theology of the Anabaptists.°

————. *Die Huterer*. Wien, 1918. Reprint available.

Wray, Frank. "Free Will, Anabaptist Position," *ME*, Vol. II (1959), pp. 387-389. Additions by H. S. Bender.

Yoder, Jess. "The Franckenthal Debate with the Anabaptists in 1571," *MQR*, XXXVI (1962), pp. 14-35; 116-146.

Yoder, John H. *Täufertum und Reformation in der Schweiz.* Vol. I, *Die Gespräche zwischen Täufern und Reformatoren, 1523-1538* (Schriftenreihe des Mennonitischen Geschichtsvereins, Nr. 6). 1962.

————Vol. II: *Täufertum und Reformation im Gespräch. Dogmengeschichtliche Untersuchung der frühen Gespräche zwischen Schweizerischen Täufern und Reformatoren,* Zürich, 1968. A systematic interpretation of implied theology.

————. "Binding and Loosing," in *Concern*, No. 14, 1967, pp. 2-32. A pamphlet series for questions of Christian renewal, available from Mennonite Publishing House, Scottdale, Pa. The same issue contains also further material concerning church discipline.°

INDEX

Topics, Persons, and Places

ROBERT FRIEDMANN
1891-1970

Dr. Robert Friedmann served in the Austrian army from 1914-18 near the Italian front. These four years radically changed Friedmann's life. His scholarly interests turned from engineering to history, his faith from Jewish to Christian.

In 1923, following doctoral studies in history, Friedmann began his life-long study of Anabaptism. He was one of a small group of historians who set down a projected series of Anabaptist source material publications (the Täuferaktenkommission).

In 1934 Friedmann was baptized into the Christian faith. In 1939 political circumstances forced him to leave his Vienna home. Dean H. S. Bender persuaded Friedmann to move to Goshen, Indiana, where the most extensive collection of Anabaptistica in the world was housed. From 1941-43 Friedmann organized and researched the Mennonite Historical Library, and completed his *Mennonite Piety Through the Centuries* (1949).

In 1945 Friedmann accepted a professorship at Western Michigan University, Kalamazoo, Michigan, although he continued his intense Anabaptist research for another quarter century. In addition to his books and many essays, Friedmann contributed two hundred articles for the *Mennonite Encyclopedia*.